STAMPS
for the
INVESTOR

by

T. N. Trikilis

Cornerstone Library
Published by Simon & Schuster
New York

Copyright © 1981 by T. N. Trikilis
all rights reserved
including the right of reproduction
in whole or in part in any form
Published by Cornerstone Library
A Simon & Schuster Division of
Gulf & Western Corporation
1230 Avenue of the Americas
New York, New York 10020

Manufactured in the United States of America

10 9 8 7 6 5 4 3 2 1

Library of Congress Cataloging in Publication Data

Trikilis, Ted.
  Stamps for the investor.

  1. Postage-stamps—Collectors and collecting.
I. Title.
HE6213.T74   769.56′   81-7809

ISBN 0-346-12512-X   AACR2

I would like to dedicate this book to Dr. Oscar Rouck, a philatelist for over fifty years, without whose experience I would never have been made aware of the vast investment potential that the stamp world holds.

It is his love for stamps and his awareness of the economics of the world that opened my eyes to the enjoyment of stamp investing.

Thank you, Uncle Oscar,
Ted

CONTENTS

PREFACE

What makes one person a collector and another one an investor? Knowledge and street smarts! This book will try to give you both.

Although there are twenty million stamp collectors in the United States alone, very few of these "collectors" have any real understanding of the stamp investing world. As collectors, they invest hundreds of millions of dollars in postage stamps that are worth less and less every day because of runaway inflation. This book will show how to invest wisely in stamps—how to buy and sell the right stamps and how to determine their true value.

This book is for the doctor, dentist, accountant, lawyer, business person, blue- and white-collar worker who has been discouraged by the stock market and seeks a better way of keeping what they have—without suffering the penalties of taxes and inflation.

ACKNOWLEDGMENTS

I would like to express my special thanks to H. R. Harmer and Keith Harmer of Harmers of New York for providing assistance in obtaining the photographs of the rarities of the Alfred H. Caspary Collection.

I would also like to thank Robert A. Siegel of Robert A. Siegel Auction Galleries for the photographs taken from their "Rarities of The World" sale on April 5, 1980, in which the rarest stamp, British Guiana, 1856, 1¢ magenta was sold.

Some of the prices realized as stated in this book of the rarities sold between July 1, 1979, through July 1, 1980, were taken from this particular auction.

I would also like to acknowledge the Scott Publishing Company of New York for the use of their numbering and identification system in illustrating the many statements that I have made throughout the book; also for the use of their catalogue prices taken from recent published additions presently being sold on the market today.

Additional thanks to Robert E. Lippert Auctions of St. Clair Shores, Michigan, for their contributions to the photographs featured in the book.

STAMPS
for the
INVESTOR

BASIC INVESTMENT FACTS

O ver the last ten years, more people have been concerned about inflation than any other national problem. This is because it affects more people in the place where it hurts them the most—their pocketbooks.

When foreign imported oil rises in demand, it is almost always followed by an increase in price. That means that average workers will pay more of their income into that area which they use the most—entertainment or necessity with regards to the automobile. Therefore, it becomes necessary to ask for a raise to compensate for the increase, and in return, this means that the companies for which they work also must increase the cost of their product to compensate for the raise they give to their employees. And this continues until the circle of economics is complete. While this is a very simpie explanation to a basic problem, the answer is never quite so simple. The dollar continues to buy less and less, and the value of everyone's savings continues to go down and down.

This is the problem facing many people thinking of retirement several years from today. What will be the buying power of the dollars that they are saving when the time comes to use them? As people think of retirement, many never realize that the dollars put into a savings account never grow as well as or in proportion to the inflation factor of the economy.

A $10,000 balance in a savings account will earn, in one year at 6% interest, only $600. If you are only in a 25% tax bracket, you will pay $150 to Uncle Sam in income tax. Therefore, your net result of $450 will leave a gross balance of $10,450. But if inflation were only a modest 5%, your buying power at the end of that year would only be $9,927.50. So as you can see, your gross is really worth $72.50 less than it was a year earlier! Anyone wishing to retire at the age of sixty-five should be aware of the fact that Social Security may not be in existence when you are ready for it. While the government contends that it is addressing itself to the problems of inflation, the wise investor realizes that money, like manure, must be spread around to benefit from it.

There are many ways to hedge against inflation. Banks, bonds, and Savings and Loan Associations are probably the worst. While there is very little risk in this type of "investment," the gain cannot be greater than that of inflation. Banks and Savings Associations take your money and loan it to other people in order to make a profit to pay for their overhead and stockholders' dividends. They would not be able to pay for their expansion without profits. While paying you 4% to 6% simple interest, they loan it out to businesses at 8% and up for return on their loans. Why not try to get as much, if not more, for your money than the banks will get for it?

Municipal bonds can be very risky. Perhaps you remember what nearly came to pass in New York City. If it were not for federal and state help, many people would have lost their life's savings. Be sure to check every avenue when you consider investing in any city system. That which appears to be very strong on the surface just might have a very weak

foundation. Know why the money is being bor-
rowed.

If you feel that you have the time to investigate
other avenues of investing your money, you may
find a great deal of pleasure and satisfaction in doing
so. A list of interesting areas to consider is as follows
(remember, this is not in their order of preference):

- Gold and Silver
- Antiques
- Original Art
- Coins

- Oriental Rugs
- Diamonds
- Rare Stamps

GOLD AND SILVER

Gold and silver have their ups and downs (based
upon stock market conditions and foreign influence
with regard to the American dollar). Buying gold
and silver commodities can be very risky. It is like
buying stock in the stock market. If you buy in at
the proper time, you have an excellent chance to
make a good profit. But remember, with the new
tax laws governing the amount of time needed to
declare the gain as a capital gain, you also run the
risk of losing your profit either by high taxation or
by a reversal in the gold and silver market. It is true
that any loss is deductible from earned income, but
the idea of investing is to be assured that you will
have your savings grow in proportion to inflation
and not diminish, so as to create a tax shelter. Retir-
ing people do not need tax shelters unless the investments are earning more than they need to earn.
(And if this were happening, you would not neces-
sarily be reading this book.)

If you are swift enough to keep up with the gold
and silver trends, you might enjoy this quick-paced
rat race. But if you cannot devote the proper time to

read, observe, and research the gold and silver market, you are better off to place your hard-earned money into a less questionable investment that is sure to grow and that requires very little decision-making.

Gold and Silver Pitfalls

Gold and silver are both very difficult to transport from one location to another in large quantities. To risk transportation from one country to another by airplane involves the chance of being discovered by metal-detection equipment in security areas which are mainly in existence to find weapons. Trying to pass such thorough inspection is very difficult, if not impossible, to say the least.

Another pitfall is lack of earning power in a depressed gold and silver market. In March, 1980, prime interest rates reached $19\frac{1}{4}\%$ and money markets were paying short-term investors in excess of $16\frac{1}{2}\%$ interest for their money. Many gold and silver holders who were fortunate enough to have bought their gold or silver prior to March, 1979, were now able to sell their holdings and pay capital gains taxes in April, 1981. But prior to paying, they could invest their profits plus their original investments in the metal into this high-interest-paying money market and earn while waiting to pay. But what about the "suckers" who were drawn into the gold and silver hype of December, 1979, when gold hit $850 per ounce and had to continue to support their investments in the face of a very fierce declining market in March, 1980? (Gold hit $460 per ounce in March and was still falling!)

Gold has to be kept in safety deposit boxes and cannot earn interest, so it is not considered an investment with "dividends or interest." This is another pitfall to the market in gold and silver.

ANTIQUES

Antique furniture can be a very good investment, especially for young newlyweds. An antique in furniture is usually considered to be anything that is more than 100 years old. Today, though, some turn-of-the-century pieces are being rapidly gobbled up as the sources for older furniture are diminishing. Usually oak and maple furniture are primarily the mainstays of the furniture of the early 1900s.

An average person will buy several pieces of furniture during a lifetime. In most cases, they will continue to replace worn-out pieces with newer, up-to-date styles, so as to be in keeping with the modes of today. Some furniture such as sofas and arm chairs is usually more comfortable than antique pieces (having more padding and backing than normally found in older pieces). These types of pieces are exceptions, and, in my opinion, are not the types of antiques that I would recommend as investments. However, a delicate walnut or cherry nightstand or end table not only displays a great deal of warmth and coziness, but as time passes, the original purchase price will continue to rise far ahead of inflation. A new walnut-veneered cupboard will cost $1,500 or more if it comes from a reliable manufacturer, yet ten years from now you would be lucky to get $500 for it at auction or a yard sale. A good wall cupboard dating from around 1860 made of walnut or cherry wood might cost approximately the same amount of money (price depends upon condition and the dealer's need for working capital at the time). The antique cupboard will be worth at least double (or $3,000) in 1988, and not only will you have had the pleasure of using it, but your $1,500 investment will be worth much more than if the money were banked at 6% simple interest per year! The worn look of a very good antique can often add value to the piece.

One recommendation I would make is to first read as much as possible about the varying qualities of antiques before you begin to buy. Then, travel to antique dealers in your area and compare prices to get a general feeling of the retail market prices, and also to ascertain exactly what style or period of antiques you wish to buy. Do not be afraid to ask questions or inquire about prices. Many dealers will dicker with you on their posted prices, and you will not save money if you do not ask. You should also watch the newspapers for notices of house, farm, and estate auctions.

As in every business that deals in valuable commodities, there are people and dealers who often represent pieces as antiques when they are merely reproductions of originals. *Beware* of the very good "deal." The tricks are many, and even experts are often fooled by the techniques developed to trick the new investors in this market. You might try to find a reputable dealer in your area who has been in business for a while. Chances are the dealer has built up a reputable business from being fair with his customers, and you may be able to work the dealer closer to his cost if he knows that you are a serious investor.

If a good antique piece is purchased early in your investing career, you will strive to improve upon it. Do not buy pieces that have undergone extensive repair work or of which major parts have been replaced. Should you find a better piece later, you can purchase it and replace your earlier piece and perhaps show a profit in doing so. All you would have to do is advertise the replaced piece in the classified section of your local newspaper, and you will be surprised as to how many other people are doing exactly what you are doing.

Buying antiques is not only a good investment, but hours of fun. It can be a very good hobby, especially if you enjoy refinishing furniture. Many fine pieces are often bought at a steal, as paint and old varnish often hide the true quality of the wood beneath, and in some instances even hide the fact that the article is an antique. So be well read and try to learn about the basic elements concerning antiques.

Antiques Pitfalls

You can only have so many antiques in your home before they make it look like a cluttered museum. The storage of these pieces is very difficult, and the transportation can be very exasperating if the articles are large and cumbersome.

Antiques are also difficult to sell unless you find the right buyer with tastes similar to your own. Trying to take them from one country to another can also be hazardous in times of emergency. Think about the Iranian crisis and what might have happened if your total wealth were tied up in furniture in that country at the time of its happening. Would they (the Iranians) have let you ship your furniture out of the country when the United States couldn't even get its hostages back?

ART

As the world of art is constantly changing, so is the risk of buying it. I do not recommend buying modern art as an investment. On the other hand, if you truly like the work, then buy it for its aesthetic value. If you are lucky enough to see your art purchase rise in value, then you will have the enjoyment of seeing your tastes rewarded. But if the work remains relatively unknown, then it will still be worth what you paid for it, and the personal satisfaction of viewing it will never diminish.

Investing in "Old Masters" is always a wise decision. But those doing it are probably not reading this book. They probably have millions, and people to manage their millions for them. Occasionally at antiques auctions you may be "lucky" enough to find a very good piece, but you must search continuously, as others are also always doing this.

The art market is very long range as far as investments are concerned. Very rare works require a great deal of insurance and protection. Protection from the elements as well as the thief are both required. There is a certain amount of inconvenience in art investing. But to the individual who is knowledgeable, the rewards can be most gratifying.

Always keep in mind that there are hundreds of thousands of aspiring young artists, self-taught or graduating yearly from colleges and art schools. The availability of original art is greater than the availability of the buyers. Without proper promotion, critics backing them, exposure, and a great deal of luck, many artists have resigned themselves to being discovered "after their lifetime." This is usually the case with the world of art. This would also mean that your investment would not mature until that time, and obviously it would not have any real value to you if you were to retire prior to that time.

People should consider investing in art through reliable dealers only, or they should buy art for the fact that is is something that they like. Overpaying for modern art is like putting money on a crap table in Las Vegas. You are hoping for a winner, but there is just as much chance that you might have a loser—and if you can't afford to lose (in Vegas or the art world), you should not be there at all.

Art Pitfalls

A major problem in collecting art is counterfeiting. Lithographs can easily be copied and signatures

faked. Even certificates can be forged to appear better than the original documents! Many new dealers
are as new to the game of selling prints as you may
be to the buying of them. Oil paintings can be so
well counterfeited that the galleries often sell them
to reputable museums, and not until years later are
the forgeries discovered. Etchings can be struck
from existing plates and limited editions can be
numbered so as to duplicate a print and number so
effectively that even the real artist could not tell the
difference.

COINS

An investment very similar to stamps is coins. Just as
there are quite a few countries that have minted
stamps, there are many more that have minted
money. The potential areas of investment in the
coin world are almost infinite. Coins were used as a
medium of exchange long before the printing press
was even invented.

The first advice I would give to prospective coin
investors is to specialize. Not only specialize in a
country, but in a specific time period. Rare coins can
appreciate as well as stamps, but coin condition is
much more difficult to ascertain than is the condition of stamps. Grading can be debated for hours
even among seasoned coin investors. A "very fine"
circulated coin may be considered "extremely fine"
circulated, and this could affect the cash price by
10% to 15%. Many coin investors buy only gold
coins as protection against a faulty market. The
price of gold can determine the value of a coin if the
weight of the coin is greater than the catalogue value of it.

Coins present a problem if one considers ever taking his investment out of the country. Many metal
detectors can find the coins without a thorough

search. While coins can be considered in the same vein as bearer bonds, paper cannot be detected, while coins can easily be detected and confiscated.

The stamp investment illustrates how money can be transferred from one country to another without penalty of currency exchange. Many foreigners take their investments out of their country in the form of stamps when the economy is uncertain due to governmental problems. Coins, on the other hand, may not increase in value proportionally with stamps. Many more people used money long before postage stamps, and therefore more of it was created to meet the public need.

Coin Pitfalls

Because of their weight, semi-precious coins (valued between $100 and $250) may weigh quite a bit if a $50,000 cash equivalent was to be taken out of a country. They would be difficult to carry on your person, and the storing of the coins in your luggage would certainly draw attention at the airport security gates.

ORIENTAL RUGS

The Oriental rug has always been a "good" investment, but not until the last five years has it been a "great" investment.

In the past, women and children were largely responsible for the manufacture of these celebrated rugs. All bona fide Oriental rugs were made by hand, and every one of their millions of knots was tied separately. Hundred of man-hours went into designing and producing woolen and silk rugs of the very highest quality which would last for generations and, if properly cared for, for hundreds of years. The color is created by ancient dyeing methods handed down from generation to generation.

Certain types of knots are characteristic of particular geographical areas. With all these factors in mind, it is not hard to see why collecting Oriental rugs resembles collecting art.

But conditions change rapidly. Consider, for example, the late Shah of Iran's decree to the effect that no child under the age of eighteen should work in the rug factories tying knots. The outcome of this edict has been twofold. On the one hand, children in Iran no longer develop deformities of the hand, and they go to school instead of tying knots. At the same time, few rugs are being made and the cost of labor, now supplied by adults, has skyrocketed. The rugs themselves have naturally escalated rapidly in value.

There are many factors to consider when investing in rugs. First, how fine is the rug? This is usually determined by the number of knots per square inch. Also, the material used is a factor. Silk, being the finest fiber, will allow more knots to be tied per square inch than wool or cotton. Wool is the next best material, as it will wear better than cotton. Cotton is often associated with reproductions and cheaper import "Orientals" from other countries not well known for this art. Beware of the cotton Belgium reproductions that are machine-made and of the Oriental design! Rugs extremely worn or damaged are worth only a slight fraction of a fair rug in moderate condition. Basic things to consider when buying rugs are: 1. *number of knots per square inch* (the more the better); 2. *color*—sharp, clear, well-defined color (unless a particular tribe has unique color pattern); 3. *age*—the older the rug, the higher the value (some antiques are priceless); 4. *type and size of knots*—some kinds of knots are no longer being tied, and these rugs are considered rare; 5. *size of rug*—while many smaller rugs will sell for more than larger rugs, it is usually because of factors 1 through 4, but very large rugs are harder to make, and if you can combine 1 through 4 with size, you will have a very valuable article; 6. *condition*—remember, if it is worn, extremely faded, repaired, or has holes in it, *it is not a good investment, generally speaking!*

My best advice for the potential rug investor is to read as much about Oriental rugs as possible and perhaps take a college course in the subject before making any buys. Also, go to the rug dealers and auctions before you buy and compare prices. Try to appraise the market before you invest.

Oriental Rug Pitfalls

Too many rug investors place the greater portion of their cash into large rugs (8′ × 10′ or larger). There are many reasons to consider this a pitfall, but there are rug merchants who will disagree—especially if they are sitting on large inventories of large rugs! When it comes time to sell a large rug for liquidation of your investment, you may have to take the rug over to a prospective buyer's house so that the rug can be seen in the environment of the buyer's room. This can be quite cumbersome, and the rug can be very heavy. There will be many more buyers available for smaller, less expensive rugs than there will be for the larger ones. Two feet by three feet and larger sizes up to four feet by seven feet are easier to carry and can easily be placed in a variety of places in most homes. These are good sizes in which to invest money, as the larger rugs are definitely much more expensive by proportion and will sit longer in your storage area than the smaller ones.

The greater the size of the rug, the greater area needed to store the rug. You cannot place the larger rugs in chests or cubbyholes to hide them from would-be thieves. The insurance for these rugs can also be a pitfall if your house is not adequately protected from this type of exposure. If your activities as a "rug investor" are well known and you advertise the fact in newspapers, many thieves will make appointments to view the rugs in your home and use this as an opportunity to "case the joint" prior to returning to rob you. So each client can be a suspect if robbery does occur.

DIAMONDS

Diamonds are a very glamorous investment and can be very profitable if properly handled. The diamond has a few benefits over gold and silver as a "small size" investment, and as a comparison to the larger investments mentioned (antiques, rugs, and original art), the size is a significant factor.

Diamonds must have a certificate with them from an authoritative source before buying occurs. The main purpose of the certificate is to grade the diamond by size, color, and clarity. It also attests to its being genuine. Many new man-made stones are similar in nature to the diamond and nearly as hard. A diamond's certificate can also record information that will describe the item in case of theft. A certificate listing the flaws or absence of them, along with the correct weight and color, is just as valuable as a photograph would be.

Always buy diamonds from dealers or brokers at a wholesale price, with a slight amount over it as commission to the seller. Too many times a "good deal" can be made on the spur of the moment, as the seller "has to sell" because the seller needs the money. Don't you believe it! There's no such thing as a free lunch. Take the time to have the diamond appraised by a retailer (for suggested retail) and an expert gemological society, notably the Gemological Institute of America (G.I.A.), the *ne plus ultra* source as far as appraisals are concerned.

If the retailer tells you that the stone has a retail

value of $3,000, divide the estimated retail value by 3. In the jewelry business, an average retailer will work on a "triple keystone" mark-up. That means that the retail price of a piece of jewelry is generally three times the retailer's cost. Therefore, the stone would have a wholesale value of $1,000. A good price would be $1,100 ($100 would be a 10% commission).

The gemological society would grade the stone and verify that it is a real diamond. The certificate would be helpful in the event that you wished later to liquidate your investment. It would also save a great deal of time, as some certificates take three to four weeks to obtain.

I would recommend only stones that are one carat or larger by weight and have no visible dark spots in the stone that can be seen with the naked eye. Try to buy those stones that appear to be white, near-white, or blue-white. Yellow-tinted stones are not as desirable and do not reflect that "fire" that a diamond is known for. The newer-cut stones are larger-appearing, as the surface of the face is broader and makes the stone look larger by weight than it really is. Older stones are deeper and are not cut to let as much light into the stone as the new shallower stones do.

If you buy the stone at a retail price, you will have to hold the stone longer than if bought at the wholesale price in order to realize a profit on your investment.

Diamond Pitfalls

A major problem with selling a diamond is finding a willing buyer. If you buy at retail, you may have to take the stone to a retail merchant in order to sell the stone. The retailer is generally buying stones from the diamond exchange or from a wholesale merchant in New York City. There the retailer can bargain with the wholesaler to get better prices, and the retailer buys when he needs something. In selling your stone to the retailer, the retailer may have just returned from a buying trip and is not in need of additional inventory unless the retailer can buy it at a better bargain than what was purchased in New York. Therefore, it would have to be below wholesale—and that would mean a loss to you!

Try to make arrangements at the time you buy the stone from a dealer or retailer to sell it back to the same place at a later date. The retailer or dealer may want it back and give you a sizable profit. Thus, you will be certain to tell friends and associates of your quick profit in the diamond market and may give the dealer or retailer numerous new customers!

As with Oriental rugs, the larger the diamond, the more difficult to find a buyer.

Another way to sell your diamond or diamonds is to advertise in the classified section of a newspaper in order to attract a young couple thinking of marriage as possible customers for your stones. Do not list your address, but use either a post office box number or a telephone number and arrange to show the diamond at a local bank so that it will appear that your valuable stones are kept in a safety deposit box. You will avoid the chances of being robbed in your home, should one of the inquirers be a potential thief.

VALUE OF THE U.S. DOLLAR
(Since 1948)

YEAR	FACE VALUE OF CURRENCY	ACTUAL BUYING POWER	
1948	$1.00	$1.00	
Jan. 1949 to Jan. 1953	$1.00	$ .902	(End of Truman's Administration)
Jan. 1953 to Jan. 1961	$1.00	$ .807	(End of Eisenhower's Administration)
Jan. 1961 to Jan. 1965	$1.00	$ .77	(End of Kennedy's Administration)
Jan. 1965 to Jan. 1969	$1.00	$ .676	(End of Johnson's Administration)
Jan. 1969 to Aug. 1974	$1.00	$ .48	(End of Nixon's Administration)
Aug. 1974 to Jan. 1977	$1.00	$ .411	(End of Ford's Administration)
Jan. 1977 to Jan. 1980	$1.00	$ .313	(During Carter's Administration)
Jan. 1980 to Jan. 1981	$1.00	$ .25	(last year of Carter's Administration)

RARE STAMPS

COLLECTING *VS.* INVESTING

As I have spent most of the preceding pages discussing other investments rather than discussing stamps, perhaps you will be able to refer to them and compare the virtues of stamp investing as you learn. Do not confuse stamp *investing* with stamp *collecting!* While both deal in the same material, stamp collecting is a *hobby* that very rarely matures into a good investment. While stamp investing can be entertaining, it will give you a tremendous hedge against inflation. While the collector works to fill his album from the newest issues to the earliest issues, the investor will buy only those stamps that appreciate the most in value over the shortest period of time. In fact, the investor may have as many as three or four of the same issue if he can purchase them at a very good price, for good investment material will rise in value far faster than common material. And if one owned ten of the same object, and that object rose in value by 35%, would not each of the other nine objects also rise in equal proportion? Most certainly they would! So this is the first basic lesson to be learned in stamp investing: duplication cannot hurt if done in a strong investing area.

The main purpose of this book is: *to inform average people about merits of stamp investing and to*

warn them of the pitfalls. Stamp investing requires
a basic stamp education and an understanding of
what makes one stamp of one issue worth more than
another stamp of a different issue; also, why the
same issue will have different cash values, even
though both appear to be identical. This book will
also attempt to give you an understanding of why
certain issues continue to escalate rapidly and why
others will only be worth face value as postage.

When should a person begin to invest in stamps?

The proper time for a person to invest in stamps is
entirely up to the individual. Each will have reason
to invest: some to form a hedge against inflation;
some to save for college or that dreamed-of business
in the future; some for retirement or for that new
house in the country; some to get out of the stock
market or the commodities market. One thing is for
sure—all want to have more in their pocket in the
future, rather than less in the future than what is in
their pocket now. (Think about it!)

Each investor must have a certain amount of
money from time to time to save for the future. A
young adult working at odd jobs prior to leaving
high school is better off putting his money into
stamps than leaving it in a savings account. But it
may be wise for you to maintain a savings account as
an intermediate holding place until enough money
may be accumulated to buy that "right" stamp.

For older people, it is recommended that a certain amount of cash be kept on hand in case of
emergency. Stamps are easy to dispose of, but in order not to sacrifice profit, the proper amount of
time to sell will ensure you of having a greater suc-
cess. This money in saving accounts cannot be considered retirement money, but rather "rainy day"
money.

What determines the value of a stamp?

The law of supply and demand will determine the value of a stamp. This applies not only to stamps of different issues, but to stamps within an issue. It was estimated by the U.S. postal authorities that in the United States alone, over 20,000,000 stamp collectors exist. Worldwide, the number could be three to four times this amount. So if one particular issue had only 1,000,000 stamps minted, 1 person out of 20 in the United States could possibly own it. The more collectors who exist in proportion to the amount of stamps in existence of an issue will cause that issue to be worth more than an issue which has more stamps minted than the number of collectors.

Within an issue, certain stamps will be worth more than others of the same issue for the following reasons:

- Centering of the stamp's design
- Used or unused (mint)
- Physical condition of the stamp
- Error (printing mistake in color or design)
- Number of remaining stamps believed still to be in existence

As the book progresses, I will try to explain each area and show its particular relationship to the others. All of the characteristics are important, and slight variations within each category will influence the value of a particular stamp. Some are not so important as others, but the wrong evaluation can mean the difference between gaining or losing.

What is a stamp catalogue?

A stamp catalogue is a book which has much information about stamps, plus an average price index of every issue based upon current market averages obtained by the printing company at the time of the catalogue's issuance. Many catalogues are printed only once a year, and certain issues may rise during the year immediately after the catalogue's release. Therefore, the market condition may be considerably higher than the catalogue price.

There are many types of catalogues used by stamp investors and collectors. The prices may fluctuate from 10% to 20% among them. The catalogue preferred by most United States collectors and investors is *Scott Standard Postage Stamp Catalogue*. *Scott's Specialized Catalogue of United States Stamps* is additionally recommended because it will also have a section devoted to special issues and printing information. Also, it will tell you how many of an issue has been released, and give methods to identify common issues from similar, rarer designs.

Remember, the price in the catalogue is an average price of that issue in its average condition. If the stamp is in its original post office condition—unused, perfectly centered, no blemishes or faults, original gum, unhinged—it will be worth two to three times the catalogue value. Likewise, if it is off-centered, creased, has no gum, it may only be worth 20% of the listed catalogue price.

For general purposes, I find *Scott's Specialized Catalogue of United States Stamps* to be nearly 90% accurate for U.S. averages in the present stamp market. There will always be stamps that rise in value without consideration for inflation. These are the stamps that are "discovered" by dealers and collectors to be worth more than average market pricing. The popularity of these stamps is sometimes "localized" and will increase because that particular geographical area is extremely interested in obtaining that particular issue. The smart investor will refrain from this type of speculation, because it is as risky as placing your money in the stock market; unless you get in at the "right time," you may find your efforts less than rewarding. The intelligent investor should place his money in "rarer," more reliable issues; these have proven to be consistent in their growth, and, to my knowledge, have never been reduced in their value. The types of rare stamps suggested for investments will be discussed at a later chapter.

For examples in this book, I will use Scott identification numbers and prices in referring to specific issues of U.S. stamps.

What is a "rare" stamp?

The "rare" stamp has always been a prize held in value by both the investor and collector alike. A rare stamp is one that is very limited in quantity or quality, usually created as a limited edition or by a printing error not caught at the time of its printing. In the Columbian issue, the dollar issues are considered somewhat of a rare issue, as one must remember that the issue was released in 1893. During this time very few people were using $1, $3, $4, and $5 stamps. While the 2¢ issue was produced in almost 1,500,000,000 quantity (I repeat—*billion!*), the dollar issues were printed as follows:

$1—55,050 #241
$2—45,550 #242
$3—27,650 #243
$4—26,350 #244
$5—27,350 #245

With this simple illustration, you can see that the 1980 Scott catalogue value of the Scott #231 is $21 each, while the #245 is $3,100 each. Yet, based upon my statement, you would assume that the #244 should be more expensive than the #245, since there were 1,000 fewer stamps printed. This is not the case (even though it should be so!), because the #244 is the $4 stamp, and the #245 is the $5 issue. The only reason I can see why it is so is that most collectors prize the $5 issue more than the $4 issue; thus, it would have more value. (The 1980 Scott catalogue price of the $4 mint #244 is $2,850.)

Another reason there are limited editions is the proofing policies of the early years. At that time, little control was exercised in the releasing of new issues. If a new paper was tested with a new issue, the stamps were not always destroyed, but used by the postal department. If a new shade of blue ink was tested, a similar situation prevailed.

With the introduction of the two-color stamp, the printing error was born. The first real printing error was created in the "Pictorial Issues" of 1869. In the 119, 120, and the 121 issues, the second color was placed on the sheets upside down. Therefore, the "centers" of the stamps were "inverted." These inverted stamps were given their own Scott catalogue numbers 119b, 120b, and 121b. These stamps were not immediately discovered at the time of their release, and many of these issues were actually placed on covers and mailed throughout the world. No one knows exactly how many stamps are in existence, and old envelopes should be closely observed when finding one of the "Pictorial Issues" on covers (especially if found in an old attic trunk). An example of the value of these particular issues is as follows:

1978 Scott Catalogue Value:

	#119	Mint—$300	Used—$45
Inverted Error	#119b	Mint—$60,000	Used—$8,000
	#120	Mint—$700	Used—$225
Inverted Error	#120b	Mint—$40,000	Used—$7,000
	#121	Mint—$675	Used—$100
Inverted Error	#121b	Mint—$50,000	Used—$25,000

As you can see from my illustrations, the regular issue as compared to the "rare" issue is much smaller in value. Yet, at auction, one rare issue might sell for a considerable amount more than a similar issue. This brings me to the second reason that I mentioned in the beginning of this question: *quality!*

The quality of a stamp may determine the value difference between two identical stamps of the same issue. If the catalogue gives one a general average of the "market" price of the particular issue in an "average condition," then any stamp that is "better than average" in condition would be worth more than this "market price," and any that is "worse than average" would be worth less.

Certain issues are well known to the "specialist" as stamps that were printed basically "off center." If one studies the issues of investment concentration, one realizes that a well-centered issue of a generally off-centered stamp is truly a good find and investment. As far as collectors are concerned, well-centered stamps (Very Fine and Extremely Fine) are more desirous than lesser-centered stamps; and, should the time come to liquidate your holdings, these stamps will have greater demand than the Good-, Very Good-, or Fine-centered stamps. When the time comes for investment suggestions, I will explain the pros and cons of buying either of the two groups that I have discussed in this paragraph. At the present time, I would recommend that you, as a novice stamp investor, refrain from making any decision until you have read this entire book.

In addition to the centering of the stamp, one should consider the condition of the physical aspects, also. Is the gum original? Is the stamp free of creases or scrapes? Is the color sharp and bright? Is the stamp faded? Is there a natural speck of paper in the design that is visible to the eye? Many of these questions can cause the value of a stamp to decrease

10% to 20% depending on the severity of the imperfection. All of the faults would make even a "rare" stamp totally worthless, and therefore a "space filler." Do not discount the value of a "space filler" as having no intrinsic value. The stamp collector will gladly buy a space filler for his album simply because he might never otherwise fill that space with a good-quality stamp of the same issue. If you can buy space fillers at the "right" price, you can realize a good financial gain year after year in your investment. For, as the value of a "rare" stamp increases each year, does not the value of a lesser-quality stamp increase proportionately?

The rare stamp is always in demand, and even to the collector it is a prize that each strives to obtain. Whether the stamp is of "poor" quality, or of "great" quality, the desire is there. And once the collector gets his first exposure to a rare issue, the desire becomes stronger to own more! Even children at an early collecting age become aware of the value of a good collection and desire the more expensive issues. Many older collectors acquire the later issues to "show off" their real prizes. Their real desires are often hidden by the inexpensive parts of their collection. Do not fall captive to this plight! Keep your investment goals in mind at all times!

What is a "gem" stamp?

A "gem" stamp is similar in nature to a gemstone. It is the stamp that is perfect in every respect. All it needs is just one blemish to remove it from this prized classification. A "gem" stamp must have: 1. perfect centering; 2. all perforations intact and fully visible; 3. excellent color, appearing as fresh as the day it was minted; 4. never-hinged original gum; 5. *all* of #1–4—plus *no* faults!

What is a "space filler"?

A "space filler" is a badly damaged stamp that for all basic purposes has no intrinsic value. To a collector, it is usually a very expensive stamp that he may never be able to acquire because the cost would be prohibitive. Yet a damaged copy could be acquired to "fill that vacant space" still void on the stamp album's page.

What is a "counterfeit" or "fake"?

A "counterfeit" or "fake" stamp is one that has been purposely created to falsely represent a stamp that was legally minted. It is, in most cases, done of a rare issue that is very expensive and popular. There are instances in which the counterfeiter has done inexpensive issues as a "challenge" to test his ability. Some counterfeits are so well done that even philatelic experts have been fooled by their quality. When purchasing a rare stamp that has a tendency to be counterfeited, always insist upon a Philatelic Foundation Certificate for verification of its authenticity.

Where can I have a stamp authenticated?

Both the American Philatelic Society and the Society of Philatelic Americans have facilities for verifying stamps. Their addresses are listed later in this book. The Philatelic Foundation Expert Committee, 99 Park Avenue, New York City, New York 10016, does a great amount of authenticating difficult issues. They can be relied upon to give sound, accurate advice and expert opinions.

What is a "unique" issue or stamp?

u-nique (yoo-nēk) adj. 1: being the only one of its kind; sole; single; 2: being without or having no equal or like; singular.

By definition, one can easily see that a unique stamp or issue is extremely rare and is only one of a kind. The value of this item is always extremely high. When the first sheet of the ever-famous Inverted Air Mail issue was discovered in 1918, the inverted issue in its intact form was a unique issue. As there were 100 stamps in the sheet, it was later sold and separated into several singles and a plate block. The singles, though very rare, would not be unique by themselves. On the other hand, the remaining plate block would remain unique.

Another unique stamp would be the British Guiana of 1856. It is the world's rarest stamp. Since it is the only one known to be in existence, it is unique.

In a later chapter I will give brief histories of several rare and unique stamps.

What country should I collect?

The first thing to be determined is the area of investment that one should endeavor to cover. You cannot buy every stamp from every country in the world; there are just too many issues one must research before making a sound investment. The best advice I can give is to specialize in a country in which the economy is stable. This would mean a country where the currency cannot be destroyed by government overthrow or near-bankruptcy. Also consider a country that has sound growth and a gross national product that is steady and of which the world is in need. Generally, the following countries are sound investment possibilities: Great Britain, France, Switzerland, Austria, Canada, Germany, Japan, China, Spain, the Netherlands, Belgium, and the United States.

The best investment is placed in the country that will be easiest to liquidate without sacrificing profit. If you live in the United States, the demand for United States stamps is greater here than it would be in Great Britain or France. The demand for British stamps is greater in England than it is in the United States or Germany. The demand for stamps indigenous to a particular country is always greater in that country than any other part of the world. If you are a world traveler, you may benefit from your travels. You can buy United States stamps in foreign markets for less than what they sell for here in the United States. Bringing U.S. stamps into the United States is not illegal, and if the proper purchase is made, a profit of 10% to 20% might be realized within the week that might pass from the time stamps are purchased to the time they are brought into the country. Likewise, a British purchase here might bring a handsome profit in England in a similar amount of time.

One should also limit the area within a country in which investments should be placed. You cannot buy, nor should you buy, every issue minted by a certain country.

I invest only in United States stamps, so I limit my areas to the following issues: Scott catalogue numbers 1, 2, 112–122, 238–245, 290–293, 287–299, 325–327, C1–C6, C13–C15, C18, and rare blocks and inverts. The main reason I have selected these areas is because of their popularity among collectors and the stamps' sharp rises percentage-wise in value. The commemoratives are limited in the amount produced, and the availability is great at the present time. I try to stay away from stamps that have color variations because they are extremely difficult to verify unless a Philatelic Certificate accompanies it. The difference in a Scott #28 red/brown, type-I mint at $800 and a 28A Indian-red, type-I mint at $4,000 is *$3,200 (Scott's Specialized Catalogue of United States Stamps, 1978 edition)!* As you can understand from this example, if you are the slightest bit color-blind, you might make a bad guess in that area as experts often do. The issues that I have mentioned in which I invest are not generally significantly reliant upon color for correct identification. There may be color differences, but not enough to make major errors in purchasing the stamps.

When collecting foreign stamps, always bear in mind that, like anything of value, the thief or counterfeiter is always present, so beware. Many foreign stamps were counterfeited the day the real ones were minted. Even inexpensive issues have been copied as a challenge to the counterfeiter's talents. The Japanese issue have many counterfeits in their early issue. Some are so good that the originals have often been mistaken for the counterfeit issues when compared next to each other.

If you chose to invest in United States stamps, I recommend buying *Scott's Specialized Catalogue of United States Stamps.* Read it as you would a textbook. Pay particular attention to the different dies and "secret marks" section. After studying the current issue, go to a stamp dealer's showroom and observe past issues of the same catalogues. Check the different increases in prices of the many issues I have mentioned in this chapter. *Harris Catalog of Postage Stamp Prices for the U.S., United Nations, Canada and Provinces* is a U.S. price index of all U.S. stamps. This paperback shows the Scott prices from their 1950, 1960, 1970, 1975, and 1977 catalogues. It also shows the percentage of increase from 1975 to 1977. This is for both mint and used stamps, and, when available, for plate blocks.

You can also purchase from several large retailers their price lists of available stamps. You can purchase their stamps directly from them through the mail. Many local dealers also carry these retail price books and use them in determining the retail value of their inventories in their stores.

As an international traveler, are there any advantages in investing in stamps?

Many countries that have unstable governments or shaky economies often have residents wishing to take cash out of their market and place it into a stable market—someplace where the money is safe and can easily be obtained in times of emergencies.

If you were planning to take money into such a country for investment purposes, the government would hardly question the source of your money. It would simply appear and the transaction would proceed as scheduled.

But if you took rare stamps into a foreign country, the government might confiscate them. The sale of such stamps to their citizens would enable the citizen to leave their country and take these "bear bond-types" of tiny pieces of paper to a thriving stamp-purchasing country and convert them into cash again.

The seller can often receive 10% to 20% premium prices over the stamps' original purchase prices, depending on the stability of the country and the manner in which the buyer acquired the currency for which the exchange is being made.

The greater the need to take the money out of the country or to "hide the cash" in an extremely appreciating article, the better the deal!

Gamblers often purchase stamps to hedge their cash winnings prior to disposing of the money. Since any winnings accrued by a professional gambler could be taxed as income, a stamp could always be sold for cash to any large dealer with "no questions asked." This is a very major problem in identifying stolen stamps once taken from a collector or investor, especially if the holdings are separated and divided into single units.

Even if the holder of a rare stamp sold it at auction without the benefit of a receipt showing where and when the article was acquired, the seller could state: "It was part of a small collection my great-grandfather left me when he died."

Who could prove otherwise?

Is there any chance left to find rare stamps in today's community?

There are still rare finds being acquired today. Many people are inheriting family heirlooms and finding old letters and documents with valuable stamps affixed to them. Any attic that has rarely been cleaned or old trunks that have never been opened can hide material that might be valuable.

It takes only one letter with an inverted stamp to make an outstanding find. Many rare stamps have been found in such a way.

Should an investor buy "gem and unique" stamps, or second-quality stamps?

Whether you are a wealthy individual or a member of the middle class, it is always best to buy top-quality stamps. The key is to buy them at below-market prices. Anytime you are involved in an auction, and you know who the dealers are, you have an excellent chance of securing topnotch material if you over-bid the dealer by a slight amount. The dealer probably has a client waiting for such material, and if the dealer is a wise person, he will make a profit of 10% or more. So you will have quality material at a fair-market price. There is, of course, a chance that the dealer may be investing some profits into inventory for sound keeping, so be careful not to exceed market price or you may not be getting as good a bargain as can be gotten in other areas.

Purchasing second-quality stamps at good prices

has more advantages than meets the eye. If you strive to always obtain top-quality stamps at below-market prices, you may find that obtaining material is a difficult venture, to say the least. Do not be discouraged, because the more you bid, the more chances you have of being successful. Yet, if you bid on second-quality stamps at below-market prices, you will find much material readily available. If Scott #245 catalogues for $1,650 (mint 1979) and an above-average stamp is valued at $3,000, a below-average stamp may be purchased for $450. In 1980, the Scott #245 may increase 20% in one year (or $1,980—1980 catalogue value); then, the above-average stamp would be estimated in value to be $3,600, and the below-average stamp of the same issue may proportionately be worth $540 (also a 20% increase). The best thing to remember is that somewhere between the $3,600 and the $540 is the "collectors' price range" for your holding!

Whenever you hold stamps purchased at below-market prices, you always have the opportunity to sell your material to collectors and new investors. In addition to selling your stamps to other interested individuals, there are many tax advantages in donating your collection, should you sell your other non-stamp holdings for considerable profits. You do not have to sell your entire collection to realize the best benefit from it. Before you liquidate your non-stamp investment, you should consult a tax expert to find out the advantages of donating part of your stamp holdings to a charity or non-profit organization in order to receive tax relief on the profit you will generate in the final sale of your other holdings.

As you read, I will explain in detail non-profit organization stamp donations. Also listed later on are those organizations that accept this type of donation.

Should I invest in mint (unused) or canceled (used) stamps?

While mint stamps are greater in value (in most cases) than canceled stamps, there are pros and cons to both types of investing. In the early minting of postage stamps, one must remember that the post office usually minted enough stamps to fill the needs of the mail handling. The collecting of stamps was a hobby practiced by few people. Therefore, most of the stamps minted in the early years were used on covers (letters) to pay for postage costs. This is why there are fewer mint stamps of early issues and more used stamps. It is also the reason mint early stamps are worth more than used early stamps of the same issue. Today, the post office mints hundreds of millions of stamps yearly. There are estimated to be 20,000,000 stamp collectors in the U.S. The collecting of mint plate blocks has become extremely popular. This is a big rip-off! (*See* "The Great American Rip-Off" chapter, page 94.) There have been early issues that were rarely used for postage, and the used copy is much rarer than the mint copy of the same issue. Scott #39 is such a case. In fact, when considering the Scott #39 used issue for investment, it is best to have a Philatelic Foundation Certificate accompany the stamp before purchasing the stamp. The Philatelic Foundation Certificate should always accompany any issue in which the authenticity of the issue may be questioned. This certificate will verify the stamp's color, perforation, or cancellation.

It is my firm belief that if used rare issues of very fine quality are acquired for investment purposes, they will have better growth potential than mint second-quality stamps. Auction prices have proven this over the last five years concerning the "mint" verses "used" question. There is also the fact that the price of the mint stamps is rising so quickly that collectors will have to buy good used stamps at the lower prices in order to fill the vacant spaces in their stamp albums. This will cause the used-stamp prices to rise quickly!

What dollar figure is good to consider for investment in regard to individual stamp issues?

I feel that buying a stamp valued at less than $100 is more bother than it is worth. If you set a minimum limit on the price to consider for investment purposes, you will eliminate many stamps from your realm of investments. If they haven't reached this level in value by now, the chances of having one grow greatly in the next ten years is minimal. The catalogue value and the price at which one can acquire the same issue are two different prices. If your investment grows 20% in catalogue value in one year, will not a below-market purchase of the same issue grow proportionately?

If the gain is so great in stamp investing, why doesn't everyone do it?

The answer to this question is very simple. It is like other areas regarding investments that are questioned, but never discussed. All people have the same opportunity to invest their earnings in whatever commodity they desire. Many wise investors try to educate themselves as to market conditions before taking the plunge. In the area of stamp investing, most articles written about this area are done by dealers for the expansion of the "collecting myth." There are few articles written about the stamp investing potential. This book will help explain the virtues of stamp investing and give information on the methods of obtaining stamps for exactly this purpose. Many people will enter this area without investigation. They may "get lucky" and wind up with a good investment; more power to them. But, unfortunately, most will buy without knowledge and lose their shirt before it is off their back. They will become discouraged and never attempt to enter this area of investment again. There is tragedy in this, for as a member of the stamp investing group, they would have stabilized the market and they would have helped keep the material moving in the investment community.

If you are following the stamp investing market and wish to speculate, at least do not do so blindly without regard to any of the consequences.

Never invest in new present issues of stamps of any country! I know that there are many dealers who will throw this book in the trash on reading this statement, but it is the simple truth. This buying of new material is very beneficial to dealers, many of whom make a market out of new issues, and, therefore, it would hurt their retail sales greatly if every collector read this book. But this book is expensive, and no doubt the average investor will not bother to read it. I am talking, therefore, to the serious investor.

Keep in mind that the average printing of any new issue is 150,000,000 stamps, and the chances of their investment potential is almost nil. Unless you are "lucky" enough to buy a printing error, you will be buying postage that will ultimately be used at a later date by you or by the dealer to whom you sell it. There have been sheets that have increased in value, but these are nothing but small potatoes when compared to the much more lucrative opportunities available in today's stamp market.

One thousand dollars ($1,000) of new-issue "plate blocks" purchased in June, 1980, at face value from the post office would have been worth $810 in "real purchasing power" in June, 1981, with inflation averaging 19% for the entire year.

If we look back over the past few years, we remember former President Carter's plan to reduce inflation from 6.6% in January, 1978, to 6.3% by December. By July, 1978, government officials announced that the estimated inflation rate was 10.5% for the six-month period. By December it was nearly 12%.

In 1979, the country began seeing gasoline prices soar with the new crude oil prices set by OPEC, and the Federal Reserve started to squeeze the businessmen by raising the prime interest rates, hoping to halt inflation. It didn't work! Inflation soared to a 15% average by December, 1979, with no end really in sight. The banks had contributed to the fire by causing businesses to raise their wholesale prices in order to cover the additional interest costs. Prime interest rates are still hovering around 20%.

With all the inflation, any money placed in new-issue stamps would quickly be diminished in purchasing power as a result of it.

Oh, it is true that the dealers will raise the prices of catalogue value on all new-issue material. But who does this benefit—the seller (the dealer) or the buyer (consumer)? If you are to take your mint 1950–1978 stamps to another dealer to re-buy your collection, the dealer may (if you are "lucky") give you 90% of face value, unless the dealer is "sitting" on a heavy inventory. Then the dealer may give you 50% to 65% of face value, depending on what the dealer feels the material is worth and how long it will take to use it as postage or sell it to another "stamp collector." This can be verified by reading any stamp periodical in the WANTED TO BUY section of "Mint U.S."

One of the basic reasons people do not invest in stamps is that they are already stamp collectors. Because many collectors do not have "tons" of cash to put into investment, they wait until they have enough money to buy that one "special" stamp to fill up their stamp album's page. Most collectors work from the back of the book toward the front. The collector gets today's stamps from the post office, and yesterday's issue from the dealers. Through trading with other collectors or by purchasing from mail-order auctions, they often acquire rare or hard-to-find issues at good market prices.

The investor should never acquire a stamp album! All of the stamps acquired for investment should be kept in a good-quality stock book in a safety deposit box. If this is done, the investor runs less of a risk of becoming a collector. As long as the blank spaces do not appear before the investor's eyes, the investor will not be tempted to fill out his collection. The investor should not become attached to any particular issue or stamp. When buying for investment, such attachment may influence your decision in buying a stamp for more than what the market value is worth. Also, when you come to realize part of your investment in cash, you will find it difficult to part with your stamp holdings.

The investor must begin to place a certain amount of money aside every month, regardless of whether or not a purchase is made. You have to have money available for that "right" purchase, should it come along. The investor should buy three stamps of the same issue if the price is right. Most people are not "future conscious." They do not realize that a dollar today is worth more than a dollar ten years from now. If you have a home, that has equity in it. Take the second mortgage out on it even if the interest is 10%! You get the interest as a deduction at each year's end on your income taxes, and the money invested at 20% + will not be taxed until the stamps are sold two or three or more years from now. Then it will be taxed as capital gains for only the profit!

The same reasoning is involved with whole-life insurance. You can borrow money against your policy (if there is a cash value to it) at 6% interest per year. You get the interest as a deduction and the benefit of putting your money in higher-yielding stamps without fear of losing your insurance.

One thing for sure—stamps have never gone down in value in the last ten years (investment stamps, of course!). And stamp collecting has expanded tremendously in the last ten years. As the "collecting myth" grows, so will the investing side of it. With everyone else becoming a stamp collector (not investor), the demand for your material will also become greater five years from now.

Should I join a stamp association?

I do recommend joining a recognized association for a few basic reasons. First, it will help establish you as a serious stamp person in the stamp community. As you become more familiar in the stamp world, you will have information sent to you for your constant updating regarding stamp news worldwide.

The association will also help you if you require verification of a stamp purchased from a dealer or at an auction. This is usually done at a reasonable price, and if a problem arises from its investigation, the association will help to resolve it. Most associations will not tolerate any improprieties in the stamp world.

Your association number will also give the stamp public a general idea of how long you have been involved with the stamp world. There are other benefits available, but you will have to get this information directly from the association. In the back of this book is an Appendix which will give you information for writing to each association.

What is an "auction house"?

An auction house is a business engaged in selling the "consignee's lots" to the public to the highest bidder. Generally, the auction is held in the business's own premises or in a public area such as a hotel or large reserved motel room.

Established customers are notified prior to the auction date as to what will be available, where the auction will be held, and the date of the offering.

Lots are listed in an orderly fashion and printed in an auction catalogue for prior consideration and for mail-in entries by bidders unable to personally attend. In addition to printing a written description of each stamp, the more attractive lots are photographed and placed in the vicinity of the lot in the catalogue or in a special photo section of the catalogue so that the bidder may observe the quality and centering of an above-average lot. In most cases, the physical condition of a stamp is explained in great detail, utilizing symbols and abbreviations for this purpose. There is an Appendix at the back of this book (pp. 136–138) explaining the meaning of basically accepted symbols and abbreviations. Also, I have included a Philatelic Glossary (pp. 112–135) to explain what each description and philatelic term means in simple language.

By familiarizing yourself with the basic terms and symbols, you will be able to read an auction catalogue and almost visually see the lots being offered. Generally speaking, all auction houses use the same symbols, but if a symbol appears in a catalogue that is not listed in the explanatory section in this book, look on the catalogue's front or back page for the auction house's own interpretation of its "special" symbol.

One additional point to ponder: each auction house may have a difference of opinion as to the "centering" of a stamp. A stamp designated as Very

Fine by one house may be listed only as Fine to Very Fine in another house's catalogue! Therefore, you should know which houses are liberal in their descriptions and which ones are anxious to give tight, accurate descriptions.

There is also a section in this book with the names of several auction houses and their addresses. This book in no way endorses or suggests any of the auction houses for purchasing stamps for investment. The names are presented merely as an aid for your personal consideration.

How do I establish "credit" with auction houses?

The word credit usually means thirty-day terms when purchasing anything for your ownership. In the auction house understanding, it means receiving lots prior to payment. If you are on "open account" with an auction house, it is because you have furnished adequate bank references and business references. The auction house gives you the privilege of credit so that you may inspect your lot purchases prior to payment. You generally have five days from receipt of the lots to inspect them, return those lots not properly described, and pay for only those that you retain. If you abuse your credit, the auction house may elect to discontinue credit and place you on a "payment prior to release of lots" status. Then you will be forced to pay for your lots prior to inspection. The auction house will still honor returns within five days, providing that the returns were not properly described.

Again, generally speaking, 98% of all material received from reputable auction houses are properly described. There is basically no risk involved when dealing with reputable firms.

What is a "mail bid"?

Mail bids are not public auctions, but the idea is

related to the bidding process. Some companies will prepare a listing of lots to be offered through the mail or by publishing their listing in a periodical or newspaper. There will be a closing date and an explanation of terms and symbols. The "bidder" will list those lots that he is desirous of obtaining and record the highest price that he will pay for that lot or lots. The bid will be mailed to the mail bid's address for tabulation.

In most cases the lot will be sold to the highest bidder at a slight increase over the second-highest bidder's bid. If two bids are the highest and are equal, the bidder who sent the earliest bid to the mail-bid address will "win" the lot, as that bid will have been recorded first. Some mail bids will require minimum bids in order to eliminate the not-so-serious bidders from the bidding. *Remember: read the rules and conditions set down by the mail bid's advertisement carefully before you bid!*

What is a "private treaty"?

A private treaty is the placement of a stamp or stamps with a dealer, auction house, or mail-bid house for the purpose of selling without running the risk of receiving low offers or bids at auction.

When lots are placed at auction, they may be liquidated "under the hammer" and might not realize their true profit potential. It is true that the sale is immediate, but there is the risk of losing profit for fast cash. Many estates often go the auction route because many of the heirs are impatient to settle the estate. Therefore, auction is a necessity. But if time is available, the private treaty is the best method of liquidation. The commissions can be negotiated, and the prices realized are often greater than those at an auction. But one can never determine when the stamps will be sold.

In private treaty, lots are placed on consignment

with the owner of the lots, requesting a reasonable amount for the lots. It must be in keeping with market conditions. The company holding the private treaty will publish a program or catalogue with the required descriptions and photographs and the catalogue value of the holdings. Then, with the addition of the company's commission to the amount desired by the consignor, a "firm" price will be requested to buy the lot or lots. Anyone receiving the private-treaty catalogue will have an opportunity to purchase the lots offered at the prices listed without bidding. The lots are then sold to the first person wishing to buy the lots. First come is the first served.

Remember, at auction, a collector may wish to own a stamp in the worst way. If so, your gain could be much greater than "private treaty" or "mail bid," because the auction's floor activity could become extremely heated. *But,* if the auction is slow and only investors are present, you might lose profit by taking the gamble.

How do I sell my investment once I wish to "cash in"?

There are three basic ways to liquidate your investments once you decide to get out of the market:

1. Place the collection in a private treaty with a reputable firm (*see* "private treaty" section).
2. Place the collection in an auction with a reputable auction house with a good, large clientele.
3. Advertise your collection in a stamp magazine, or list it in a classified ad in your local newspaper.

Anytime you advertise your collection, you should use a post office box for an address to discourage would-be thieves from breaking into your home to rob you. Remember, stamps are as good as bearer bonds and do not need anything for transfer of ownership. No one will generally buy a large holding without first viewing it. If you decide to sell it by yourself by means of a classified ad, always arrange with your bank to use one of its offices to show the collection to give the impression that your holdings are protected by the bank's vault. If you take your material home, you also run the risk of a natural hazard, such as a fire or flood.

I recommend the first two methods for selling your stamps. Even though the firm may take 10% of the sale price as a commission, you will have a good chance to make a faster sale than if you would try to sell it by yourself. A private-treaty commission can be negotiated with the firm, and it will try to get as much for your material as the market will bear; the firm will also benefit directly from such a sale. As for the auction houses, many major houses will accept sizable holdings, also on a negotiated commission. Generally, though, if the holdings are less than $5,000, the auction houses will not take less than their 10%. If the lots are small, some houses may even charge a "lotting fee."

What is a "lotting fee"?

Many auction houses and mail-bid firms may charge a fee for listing each lot in an auction or a mail bid. This fee is usually a flat rate per lot and is subtracted from your net after the commission is deducted from the gross receipt of the lot. It can range from 50¢ and up per lot.

What is a "lot"?

. A lot is anything from one stamp to an entire collection which has been placed for sale at an auction or through a mail bid.

Have stamp prices ever fallen in value?

Basically speaking, stamps have never fallen in

price in the United States since the crash of 1929. It is true that during some periods, the rise has not been as great as it presently is with some issues. The rarer issues have made tremendous gains, while the more common issues have been raised by dealers to stimulate the collector in order to sell the postage that the dealers had purchased earlier from the post office. The common stamps will rise in value each year, but the resale value may always be 10% less than face value. If one collector sells a collection to another collector, perhaps there may be a slight profit made in this sale. But generally speaking, it is the rarer stamps that bring the higher increases in value.

Are there market updates or newsletters available to the stamp investor?

The Scott Publishing Company has a market update to which a collector or investor might subscribe. This is a periodic report that features stamps at all levels and their increase in price. Information issued in this report is often helpful to spot stamps that are rapidly moving up in the auction market or at the retail-store level.

In its newsletter, the Philatelic International Exchange has recently started releasing an auction average based on an accumulation of several auction-house prices realized. Only very valuable issues (those that are investment-worthy) are traced, and the average price of one issue in each of three basic conditions is reported. For example, an "average" stamp is referred to as a "1.00 point stamp." A "below average stamp" is referred to as a ".50 point stamp." And an "above average stamp" is known as a "2.00 point stamp." To evaluate your own holdings, you must first evaluate each stamp on the basis of the Trikilis Index, establishing the point value in each case, and then adjust by interpolation your point average to the listed average in the P.I.E. newsletter.

The P.I.E. also suggests certain stamps from par- ticular countries which are likely to be good invest- ments and gives possible trends that might influence their rapid growth.

By continually going to retail stores or reading stamp newspapers, you can surmise from the rapid rise of the stamp dealers' prices that the issues which continue to escalate are not as numerous as one would suspect. Do not be touted by the dealers' advertisements as to what to buy.

For more information on the P.I.E.'s newsletter, write to:

> Philatelic International Exchange, Inc.
> P. O. Box 456,
> Chippewa Lake, Ohio 44215

What are the advantages of donating stamps to non-profit organizations?

There are several benefits other than the mone- tary gains one may derive from donating stamps to non-profit organizations.

While the write-off value can often be as great as 10 to 1, the recipients will appreciate the material more than you may presently realize.

There are several non-profit organizations that will accept stamp material which qualifies for tax advantages in the donation category:

- Organizations for the retired elderly, such as the Longevity Research Organization
- Veterans' rehabilitation hospitals
- Colleges
- Libraries
- Churches

Many times a stamp collection which may have a few investment-quality stamps can be purchased from a collector or at an auction. The rest of the collection may have a high retail dealer stock value that, if purchased from a dealer, would be quite expensive.

At auctions, $10,000 stamp collections (catalogue value or retail value) can often be purchased for $2,000 or less! If the collection were held for one full year, it would increase perhaps another 10% in retail value (total value now being at least $11,000, if not more).

Donation of this collection to the Longevity Research Foundation by a 40% tax-bracket person would result in a $4,400 cash return from the government. The deduction would be considered as what a person would have to pay in cash in order to acquire the same material, not what the donator actually paid one year earlier. To calculate this figure, it is safe to try to acquire stamps priced or listed in the *H. E. Harris Stamp Catalogue* or the *Brookman Catalogue,* since these books list stamps sold to collectors at regular retail prices!

The Longevity Research Foundation will distribute all stamps to retired elderly people. These people will use the stamps in their collections and advance their interest in the philatelic society. Elderly people are often neglected or totally ignored. By helping them to collect stamps, you expand their interest and allow them to mingle in a world of history and graphic beauty. Stamp collecting can also be an entertaining social event shared by many collectors, old and young alike.

There are a few IRS Appeal Court rulings that have substantiated the donations as legal and allowable. A good CPA will help you establish your deduction and defend the amount deducted on past decisions. Consult a tax attorney if any doubt exists after reading this book.

If collections are donated prior to holding them for one full year, then only your cash purchase price would be allowable as the deduction. Remember, the capital gains laws prevent premature donations and deductions at retail value. Stamps must be held for one full year!

Stamps of many countries can be purchased at reasonably low cash prices and donated to churches of the same ethnic origin. Excluding rare and valuable individual stamps, many countries' histories are visually exhibited through the graphics of their stamps.

In Germany, the stamps minted between 1900 and 1945 show not only the transition from the Kaiser's rule to Hitler's holocaust, but also the devaluation of the mark (Germany's currency) after World War I and the high inflation of the currency.

A 5-mark stamp minted prior to 1920 might have had a black overprint of 100,000,000 marks in 1923. In 1933, the swastikas were just beginning to appear in German stamps; this also marks the beginning of Hitler's influence and the rise to power of the Nazi Party.

Greek Orthodox churches would be likely candidates to receive Greek stamp collections. Russian Orthodox churches would also be amenable to donations of Russian stamp collections. Churches, as well as libraries and colleges, would be able to use the collections to illustrate historical lectures and show examples of each country's political, religious, as well as artistic views in reflecting the government's attitude at the time of each stamp's minting.

From the standpoint of disabled veterans, stamps not only help in rehabilitation if they show an interest in collecting, but many veterans can begin businesses from their wheelchairs. By accumulating stamps from donations, disabled veterans can attend stamp shows and sell their stock to stamp collectors for their hobby purposes. Mail-order business can also be conducted from their homes, thereby expanding their exposure outside their city or state.

In an Appendix (page 163), I have listed organizations and institutions which will accept stamps as tax-deductable, charitable donations.

ADDITIONAL TAX INFORMATION

Books:
Financial Management of Your Coin/Stamp Estate ($16.50), by D. Larry Crumbley, Ph.D., C.P.A. This book may be obtained from:

> Information Services
> P. O. Box 9027,
> College Station, Texas 77840

Tax Law Precedents:
Alma Piston Co. *vs.* Commissioner, 1976, T. C. Memo 1976–107, December 33,753 (m)

Walker et al. *vs.* U.S., 1969, U.S. District Court, 69 USTC 9485

Goldman *vs.* Commissioner, 1967, U.S.C.A. 6th, 388 F. 2d 476

Articles:
"The Valuation of Stamps for Charitable Contributions," by Lowell J. Myers, President of National Philatelic Institute, Chicago, Illinois 60680, in *The American Philatelist,* December, 1978

"Charitable Gifts of Stamps," by D. Larry Crumb-
ley, Ph.D., C.P.A., in *Society of Philatelic American
Journal*, April, 1980

ESTATE PLANNING

What are the benefits of using stamps?
All of us are aware of the fact that death is imminent. Though we often try to "overlook" its reality, what would happen to your wealth (regardless of its size) if you should die today? Would attorneys and tax men swarm over it like flies drawn to honey? Most definitely so. Only those wise people who plan for this reality protect the ones they truly love. I would rather have my wife protected by the excess dollars I can save from the government than to have the inheritance taxes paid to the I.R.S. go into the pocket of one of our salaried government congresspeople.

When I am gone, my wife and family will not be protected by my financial earning ability. It is up to me to "educate" them in the ways of investments and to try to give them a relative understanding of how to make money with money. And every dollar I can put into their pockets before the government gets it is seed money for their future.

Stamps help me to do this.

If an investment is made by both the husband and wife, both acquire the experience of stamp investing. Should one spouse die, the one remaining will have the knowledge of disposing of the investment without "losing" it to a shrewd dealer. Since an investment in stamps requires no "title" to establish ownership, who can say that the investment belonged to the deceased or to the survivor of the marriage? Only the survivor can tell, as "dead men tell no tales." If the survivor has even a limited knowledge of stamp investing, this can protect him against a "bad sale."

In the event the deceased wishes to leave the investment to a university or library, the survivor could do so as part of the surviving estate "in memory" of the deceased, and use this "donation" at the full "cash" market value (the value at which a retailer would sell it to a collector). By doing it this way, the survivor gets the full benefit of the donation against the yearly income tax, as well as any inheritance tax that might be jointly shared by the deceased and the survivor.

What is the benefit of a "syndicate" purchasing one stamp or a group of valuable stamps?

The syndication of a major stamp purchase has a few significant advantages.

First, it enables a group of smaller investors to pool their money and purchase a very good stamp that has the potential of rising in value very quickly and showing excellent results to its investors. A stamp purchased in this manner could not normally have been purchased separately by any one of the syndicate members. Each, therefore, will experience the greatest potential on his smaller investment than a larger investor would have experienced in a similar fashion.

An example of this was the syndicated purchase of the rarest stamp in the world in 1970 (British Guiana, 1856, 1¢ magenta). The stamp was purchased through Mr. Irwin Weinberg for a group of nine investors, with the agreement that they would hold the stamp for 10 years. Mr. Weinberg purchased the stamp for $280,000 at a time when the seller (previous owner) absorbed the 20% commission when the stamp was sold. This would have netted the seller $252,000 after commission.

On April 5, 1980, Weinberg sold the stamp for $850,000. But since his original purchase, the auction houses adopted the "European System" with regard to the cost of selling and buying stamps at auction. Now the seller and the buyer both pay 10% (they split the 20% commission) when the stamp is auctioned! Weinberg made a cool $85,000 additional profit because of this policy change, since his 10% was one-half of what it would have been 3 years ago!

Weinberg's net for his investors was $765,000! All investors would have a capital gains tax to pay on their profit (28% maximum!). Only $485,000 would be taxable, but that would be divided up among each of the investors by the percentage that each owned in the beginning of the syndication.

The second advantage of syndication is spreading the money around into a group of valuable stamps and acquiring a "portfolio" of rare investments, instead of making one huge stamp buy.

Each rare issue will grow in relationship to the inflation factor, but certain stamps, both in foreign countries and in the United States, might soar and raise the overall average considerably.

In 1979, England experienced a tremendous inflationary period. Certain mint British stamps ballooned upward fantastically. There was a growth of 90% to 110% in various issues. (Compare Scott Great Britain 1979 to Scott Great Britain 1980.)

By buying a group of different rare stamps, you can hedge your investments and average the group for overall growth potential.

How does one go about "syndicating" a stamp investment?

By inquiring among your friends and relatives, you may be able to group together enough people to make syndication worthwhile. Do not get involved with people who do not have cash to invest or who are constantly worrying about "losing their money." They will be a thorn in your side—more trouble than they are worth.

First set a figure that must be attained before syndication will begin—let us say $200,000 as a starting figure.

Then limit the amount of minimum "shares" by dividing the $200,000 into the maximum amount of individuals you would want in the syndicate—let us say 10 people at the maximum. (This could mean $20,000 per person or per "share.") There could be 6 people at $20,000 each, and 2 people at $40,000 each.

After the people have decided, each should place his money in the escrow account to be dispersed by a reliable person or institution (bank). Then an article of syndication should be drawn up by an attorney that states the irrevocable conditions under which the money will be spent for acquisition of investment stamps.

All members must sign the agreement without exceptions!

The agreement should list a date upon which the investment will be liquidated. The agreement must be binding on any heirs or successors. There can be no "earlier" liquidation date. (I recommend a 5-year minimum.) The agreement should state who shall be responsible for buying and selling the investment (an agent or auction house). The agreement must state where the investment shall be kept (a safety deposit box), with periodic inspection of material by 3 or more of the shareholders present. (This could be an annual meeting set up to review the growth at the time of a catalogue printing or a major auction house selling similar material, with prices realized by that auction house being sent to the 3 shareholders responsible for the stamp investment.)

There are many ways to skin a cat, but a good C.P.A. or attorney can suggest other alternatives to my method of syndication.

RETIREMENT
STRATEGY

With inflation still soaring at a double-digit rate, the average retirement plan or "profit-sharing program" is slowly but surely being robbed by the high cost of living.

If you are involved in a "profit-sharing program" that either you or the company for which you work has created for retirement, you have under the new I.R.S. ruling the opportunity to "suggest" where your portion of the fund should be placed in approved investments.

The average "profit-sharing" programs are controlled by insurance companies that guarantee the participants the funds at retirement age. They are usually invested in projects in which the insurance company may risk the loss, but the participant is guaranteed an $8\frac{1}{2}\%$ to $9\frac{1}{2}\%$ interest rate that is non-taxable until the money is taken out of the program at the time of retirement.

This appeared to be quite equitable in the early or mid-'70s; by the late '70s or the '80s, the value of this tax-deferrable income is not as lucrative as it must be in order to keep in pace and on par with the inflation rate.

Consider $10,000 earning 9% interest in a profit-sharing program:

The first-year earnings are $900, bringing the total worth of the program to $10,900. If inflation is

20% that year, the loss in buying power of the
$10,900 is $2,180. If you retired that year, you
would have to pay taxes on the $10,900 if taken out
all at one time, and if it were taxed at 25%, the
value of the $10,900 after taxes would be less
$2,725, or a gross of $8,175. The buying power of
the $8,175 that you would actually receive would be
20% less (the approximate inflation rate), or $6,540!

This is only a one-year projection. The following
figures illustrate the simple economics of a 5-year
profit-sharing program involving a deposit of
$10,000 per year, with an annual 9% interest pay-
ment compounded for the 5-year period. The second column illustrates the actual buying power of
the principal plus the interest at the end of year
year if inflation were a constant 20%.

ABP = Actual Buying Power   P   = Principal
I   = Interest   Inf   = Inflation
C   = Cash

YEAR 1980

1st Year	$10,000.00 - P		$10,900.00 - P&I
	+ 900.00 - 9% I		− 2,180.00 - Inf (20%)
Total	$10,900.00 - P&I Yr.		$ 8,720.00 - ABP End 1980
	End C		

YEAR 1981

2nd Year	$10,900.00 - 1980 C	I.	$ 8,720.00 - APB End 1980
	10,000.00 - 2nd Yr. P		− 1,744.00 - I on 1980
			Money
	981.00 - I on 1980		$ 6,976.00 - ABP End 1981
	+ 900.00 - I in P	II.	$ 981.00 - I earned 1980
	1981		− 196.20 - Inf on I earned
Total	$22,781.00 - P&I Yr.		$ 784.80 - ABP End 1981
	End 1981C		
		III.	$10,900.00 - P&I 1981
			− 2,180.00 - (Inf 20%)
			$ 8,720.00 - ABP End 1981

Total ABP End of 1981 (2nd Year) = $16,480.80

STAMPS FOR THE INVESTOR

YEAR 1982

3rd Year					
$22,781.00	- P&I 1980, 1981	I.	$16,480.80	- ABP End 1981	
2,050.29	- 9% I End 1982		− 3,296.16	- (20% Inf 1980)	
$10,000.00	- 3rd Yr. P		$13,184.64	- ABP End of 1982 on	
+ 900.00	- 9% I on 3rd Yr. P	II.	1980+1981		
$35,731.29	- Total Yr. End 1982 C		$10,900.00	- P&I 1982	
			− 2,180.00	- (Inf 20%)	
			$ 8,720.00	- ABP End 1982	

Total ABP End of 1982 (3rd Year) = $21,904.64

YEAR 1983

4th Year					
$35,731.29	- P&I 1980, 1981, 1982	I.	$21,904.64	- ABP End 1982	
3,215.82	- 9% I end of 1983		− 4,380.93	- (Inf 20%)	
10,000.00	- 4th Yr. P		$17,523.71	- ABP End 1983	
+ 900.00	- 9% I in 4th Yr.	II.	$10,900.00	- P&I 1983	
$49,847.11	- Total Yr. End 1983 C		− 2,180.00	- (Inf 20%)	
			$ 8,720.00	- ABP End 1983	

Total ABP End of 1983 (4th Year) = $26,243.71

YEAR 1984

5th Year	$49,847.11 - P&I 1980, 1981, 1982, 1983	I.	$17,523.71 - ABP End 1983
			− 3,504.74 - (Inf 20%)
			$14,018.97 - ABP End 1984
	6,848.17 - 9% I End 1984		
	10,000.00 - 5th Yr. P		
	+ 900.00 - 9% I in 5th Yr.		
	$67,595.28 - Total Yr. End 1984 C		
		II.	$10,900.00 - P&I
			− 2,180.00 - (Inf 20%)
			$ 8,720.00 - ABP End 1984

Total APB End 1984 (5th Year) = $22,738.97!

I have tried to simplify the illustration to show a reasonable value of cash in the bank as opposed to the actual buying power of that cash five years later. One must also consider an even smaller buying power in the case of the actual value of each $10,000 principal deposit when compared with the fifth year's deposit.

A more alarming thought is the fact that the $67,595.28 is taxable as it is withdrawn from the retirement account! There is a 5-year limit on withdrawing money at retirement age. You must take it out at the *end* of that 5-year period.

If equally averaged over the 5 years, the $13,519.05 would be taxed at a rate as if it were income in each of the 5 years. If other "outside" investments are earning income, also, your actual *cash* in hand could be considerably less.

STAMPS INSTEAD OF CASH

If you direct your portion of the profit-sharing program to be placed in good-quality, sound-investment issues of stamps, the benefits can be more than rewarding.

By attemping to place your *cash* in investment-stamp issues, such stamps will grow in proportion to the inflation rate of the economy. In the years 1975 to 1980, the popular U.S. issues of investment-quality stamps out-performed the majority of all investments, including gold and silver (excluding the fall-of-1979 push!). A rare investment-quality stamp did not fall in value during this 5-year span. In fact, not since the early 1930s has the price of a rare stamp receded from its previous established price.

The following illustration will show the value of a stamp-investment program using the average inflation rate of 20% and compare it to the liquidated value at the *end* of that 5-year period.

Usually investment quality stamps have kept a pace of almost a two to one ratio over yearly inflation. I will use a conservative 1½ times ratio or 30% to illustrate the comparison.

P   = Principal   I   = Interest
Inf. = Inflation   C   = Cash

YEAR 1980

1st Year	$10,000.00	- P in Stamps
	+ 3,000.00	- 30% Inf of Value
Total Cash Value	$13,000.00	- 30% increase in C value at End of 1980

YEAR 1981

2nd Year	$10,000.00	- P in Stamps 1981 Contribution
	3,000.00	- Inf of C value at End of 1981
	+16,900.00	- C value of 1980 Stamps ($13,900.00 End of 1980) ($ 3,900.00 End of 1981)
Total Cash Value	$29,900.00	

RETIREMENT STRATEGY

YEAR 1982

3rd Year

$10,000.00 -	P in Stamps 1982 Contribution
3,000.00 -	Inf of 1982 Stamps
21,970.00 -	($16,900.00 C value End of 1981 of Stamps purchased in 1980) ($5,070.00 End of 1982 increased C value of 1980 Stamps)
16,900.00 -	C value of 1981 Stamps ($13,000.00) ($3,900.00 Increase in C value)

Total Cash Value $51,870.00

YEAR 1983

4th Year

$10,000.00 -	P in Stamps 1983 Contribution
3,000 -	Inf of 1983 Stamps
28,561.00 -	($21,970.00 - C value End of 1982 of 1980 Stamps) ($6,591.00 - 1983 Increase in C value of 1980 Stamps)
21,970.00 -	($16,900.00 - C value End of 1981 ($5,070.00 - Increase in C value of 1981 Stamps)
16,900.00 -	($13,000.00 - C value of 1982 Stamps) ($3,900.00 - C Increase of 1982 Stamps)

Total Cash Value $80,431.00

YEAR 1984

5th Year

$10,000 -	P in Stamps 1984 Contribution
3,000.00 -	Inf of 1984 Stamps
37,661.00 -	($28,970.00 - C value End of 1983 of 1980 Stamps) ($8,691.00 - 1984 increase of C value)
28,561.00 -	($21,970.00 - C value end of 1983 of 1981 Stamp purchases) ($6,591.00 - 1984 increase in C value)
21,970.00 -	($16,900.00 - C value End of 1983 of 1982 Stamp purchases) ($5,070.00 - 1984 increase in C value)
$16,900.00 -	($13,000.00 - C value End of 1983 of 1983 Stamp purchases) ($3,900.00 - 1984 increase in C value)

Total Cash Value $118,092.00

If we consider the Actual Cash Earned from 1980 to 1984 in the first illustration of profit-sharing, we can compare the $67,595.28 Cash to Buying Power of $22,738.97.

The ratio of Cash to Actual Buying Power is $67,595.28:$22,737.97, or approximately $3 in Cash is really worth $1 in buying power as compared to the value of a 1980 dollar. A 1984 dollar is really worth only $.33 after 5 years of inflation.

Using this comparison, the Cash derived from liquidation of your stamp holdings at the end of the fifth year is $118,092.

The Actual Buying Power of the $118,092 by comparison to the above analogy is $39,364.

Illustration #1		Illustration #2
ABP of Cash - $22,739.97	X	- ABP of Liquidated Stamps
Actual Cash - $67,595.28	$118,092.00	- Actual Cash Value of Liquidated Stamps

By purchasing stamps with only a 30% inflation rate, you will wind up with $16,625 Actual Buying Dollars more in your pocket, as compared to Illustration #1.

In addition to this considerable increase in Buying Power, there are several advantages to having your retirement money in stamps as opposed to *Cash:*

1. The catalogue value will most often be greater than the "Actual Cash Value" of the investments. Therefore, you can donate the appreciation value of the stamps to non-profit organizations and claim the appraised value against the actual cash value when you liquidate (*see* List of Organizations that Accept Stamps as Charitable Donations, p. 163).
2. You will only pay taxes on the liquidated stamps *as you* liquidate.
3. The gift of such stamps can be at the cost of purchase, not at appraised value.
4. (See a C.P.A. for additional benefits!)

THE
KEOGH PLAN

If you are not part of a company's profit-sharing program, you may be eligible for your own retirement plan if it is approved by the I.R.S.

Consult your C.P.A. as to what requirements the I.R.S. sets for such a plan. Then begin acquiring the cash for such contributions to qualify for the approved plan. Rent a safety deposit box separate from your personal box and begin "investing" accrued cash into investment-quality stamps to be placed into this account's safety deposit box.

Keep accurate records as to what was purchased, what was paid for each purchase, when each purchase was made, and from whom each purchase was acquired.

Many of you can be qualified for a dealer's discount when purchasing from other retail stamp dealers, or you may find agents to represent you at auctions for a 5% commission on purchased items for your fund.

If you have the time, you can obtain material patiently by attending stamp auctions or writing in to mail-bid houses. But buy right in the beginning, or your investment will not grow for the first few years. Also, use reputable stamp agents for purchasing from stamp auction houses. Many houses will recommend agents or will represent you directly with a house person who is qualified and experienced in present market conditions.

A big advantage to having your own Keogh plan in stamp investments is the ability to buy good material for your own personal plan, then sell it to another interested party at a profit and keep the profit and principal in the Keogh plan for another better purchase.

The "parlaying" of such a nature can allow your

stamp holdings to grow even faster than the "infla-tion factor" previously illustrated. This also gives you the opportunity to upgrade your material.

There are already several individuals utilizing stamps as part of their Keogh plan, but you must qualify for the plan in order to use tax-deferred money for such purchases.

On the other hand, any stamp purchased that is not part of a Keogh plan can be considered material for retirement—especially if you are in a high tax bracket! While dividends and interest are taxed as "unearned income," your "inflation factor" cannot be taxed until the stamps are actually sold. And if sold, only the *profit* is taxable under a capital gains tax situation if the stamps are sold one year or later from date of purchase.

EVALUATING AND VALUING YOUR STAMP COLLECTION

THE TRIKILIS SYSTEM

How do I know the cash value of a stamp as compared to the catalogue value?

This is perhaps the most difficult question to answer of all the questions that this book has answered thus far. The physical appearance of a stamp may determine the difference between two stamps of the same issue by as much as 50% to 100%! You must realize that if a stamp is badly damaged, regardless of its catalogue value, that the stamp may have no intrinsic value whatsoever. If a stamp is in perfect post office condition and perfectly centered, it may be worth two to three times the catalogue value. Therefore, keeping all these points in mind, there is some way to determine the cash value of a stamp and be within the market by a plus or minus 10%.

I have a basic system that may help you in evaluating the cash value of a stamp in its relationship to market value and catalogue value. Generally speaking, most investors and collectors prefer a very well-centered stamp to one that is off center. In evaluating a stamp, start with a "zero" value. If the stamp is excessively damaged (*e.g.*, a large piece is missing), do not buy it!

Parts and Areas of a Stamp

Top

UPPER RIGHT CORNER

FACE VALUE

Right side

MARGIN

DESIGN

LOWER RIGHT CORNER

UPPER LEFT CORNER

PERFORATION HOLE

PERFORATION

Left side

LOWER LEFT CORNER

Bottom

THE TRIKILIS INDEX

Centering Value Points:

XF =	2.00 points	VG-F =	.30 points
VF-XF =	1.50 points	VG =	.25 points
VF =	1.00 points	G-VG =	.15 points
F-VF =	.75 points	G =	.08 points
F =	.50 points		

EXPLANATION OF CENTERING

G

Good (G)
(+ .08 Points)

Perforations usually touch two sides of stamp's design.

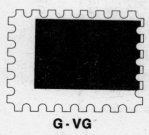

G - VG

Good to Very Good (G-VG)
(+ .15 Points)

Perforations touch design on one side and barely clear another side.

VG

Very Good (VG)
(+ .25 Points)

Perforations touch only one side of stamp's design.

VG · F

Very Good to Fine
(VG-F)
(+ .30 Points)

Perforation barely
clears on one side
of stamp's design.
Other three sides
of stamp are gen-
erous margins.

F

Fine (F)
(+ .50 Points)

Perforations clear
all sides of stamp's
design, but remain
fairly close to one
side of stamp's de-
sign.

F · VF

Fine to Very Fine
(F-VF)
(+ .75 Points)

Perforations clear
generously all sides
of stamp's design,
but one side may
appear smaller
than other three
sides.

VF

Very Fine (VF)
(+ 1.00 Points)

Perforations clear
all sides of stamp's
design generously
and appear to be
almost equidistant
all around.

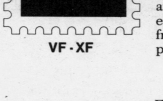

VF · XF

Very Fine to Ex-
tremely Fine
(VF-XF)
(+ 1.50 Points)

Perforations clear
all sides of stamp's
design generously
and appear to be
equidistant
from all sides of
perforations.

Extremely Fine
(XF)
(+ 2.00 Points)

Perforations clear
generously all sides
of stamp's design
and have large
wide margins all
around; perfectly
centered. (Consid-
ered a gem!)

XF

Gum Condition Value Points*:

Full Original Gum, Never Hinged	(OG, NH)	=	1.00 points (+)
Full Original Gum, Very Light Hinge	(OG, VLH)	=	.75 points (+)
Full Original Gum, Light Hinge	(OG, LH)	=	.50 points (+)
Full Original Gum Disturbed	(OG dist.)	=	.10 points (+)
No Gum	(NG)	=	.50 points (−)
Full Original Gum, Never Hinged, Natural Gum Skip	(OG, NH, NGS)	=	.65 points (+)
Full Original Gum, Hinge Remnant	(OG, HR)	=	.05 points (+)
Full Original Gum, Heavy Hinge Remnant	(OG, HHR)	=	.00 points
Regummed, Never Hinged	(RG, NH)	=	.10 points (+)
Regummed, Very Light Hinge	(RG, VLH)	=	.05 points (+)
Regummed, Light Hinge	(RG, LH)	=	.00 points
Regummed, Hinged Remnant	(RG, HR)	=	.10 points (−)

Special Note: If Full Original Gum with Natural Gum Skip has Hinge Remnant or Heavy Hinge Remnant, then point value is = .10 points (−).

Coloration:

Bright Crisp Natural Color	=	.50 points (+)
Color is Clear, But Not Bright	=	.15 points (+)
Color is Dull, Slightly Faded	=	.15 points (−)
Color is Badly Faded	=	.50 points (−)

Blemishes*:

Stains on Front or Back	1 sq. mm stain = .10 points (−)
	2 sq. mm stain = .20 points (−)
	3 sq. mm stain = .40 points (−)

Special Note: Point value increases geometrically with size; *e.g.*—4 sq. mm = .80 points (−).

Perforations*:

All Perforations Intact	=	.25 points (+)
All Perforations Intact, One Short	=	.10 points (−)
All Perforations Intact, Except One Is Missing	=	.15 points (−)
All Perforations Intact, Except Two Are Missing	=	.30 points (−)
All Perforations Intact, Except Three Are Missing	=	.45 points (−)

Special Note: Subtract .15 points for each missing perforation.

VALUING YOUR COLLECTION

MEASUREMENTS OF THINS, SCRAPES, HOLES, TEARS, AND CREASES

■ = 1 square mm
■ = 2 square mm
■ = 3 square mm
■ = 4 square mm
■ = 5 square mm
■ = 6 square mm
■ = 7 square mm

■ = 8 square mm
■ = 9 square mm
■ = 10 square mm

Thins*:

1 sq. mm Thin	= .15 points (−)
2 sq. mm Thin	= .30 points (−)
3 sq. mm Thin	= .45 points (−)

Special Note: The larger the thin, the greater the points subtracted.

Surface Scrapes*:

1 sq. mm Scrape	= .20 points (−)
2 sq. mm Scrape	= .40 points (−)
3 sq. mm Scrape	= .60 points (−)

Special Note: The larger the scrape, the greater the points subtracted!

Holes or "Breaks in Surface of Stamp"*:

"Pinhole"	= .25 points (−)
1 sq. mm Hole	= .50 points (−)

Special Note: Larger holes generally create "space fillers" only!

Tears*:

1 mm Tear	= .20 points (−)
2 mm Tear	= .40 points (−)
3 mm Tear	= .60 points (−)

*Special Note: Subtract .20 points for each mm of tear!

Creases*:

1 mm Crease	= .10 points (−)
2 mm Crease	= .20 points (−)
3 mm Crease	= .30 points (−)

*Special Note: Subtract .10 points for each mm of crease!

Stamps with Straight Edges: Subtract .20 points per straight edge!

Stamps with corners missing or "attached" with a hinge are regarded as the same as stamps with holes or "breaks" and graded as such!

Cancellation:

Light Cancel Near Corner of Stamp, Appears Mint	(VL canc.)	= .25 points (+)
Light Clear Cancellation of Unusual Shape	(L canc.)	= .15 points (+)
Light Cancellation with Special Color (See a Catalogue for Special Price)		
Heavy Cancel That Darkens the Stamp So That Design Is Not Visible	(H canc.)	= .25 points (−)

USING THE TRIKILIS INDEX

In using the Index, it is best to evaluate the stamp in question from a purely objective standpoint. Do not become over-desirous of obtaining the stamp at a "cash" loss. A good evaluation will help you realize a profit at the later time of sale when you wish to liquidate your investment. The closer you come to the actual cash value of the stamp, the greater your investment will grow in relationship to it.

EXAMPLE:

Stamp "A" catalogues at $1,000, but cash value is $200.

If you appraise it at $500, and pay $500 for it, when the $1,000 goes to $1,500 in catalogue value, the $200 will only go to $300 by proportion! You will have to wait for it to catalogue at $2,500 before another appraiser using the grade scale you have used more accurately appraises it at the 20% catalogue value!

But if you appraise the stamp at $200 and it goes to $1,500, then your investment is now worth $300 by proportion and you have *gained* 50% on your purchase!

The greatest mistake an investor can make is "liking" a particular issue so much that it interferes with his true evaluation of that issue and causes the investor to lose money before a profit can be gained.

To use the Index properly, place the stamp before you just as a doctor or biologist might position a specimen for examination. Then evaluate all the positive aspects, writing down each one and totaling the positive points of the stamp.

After the "positive" evaluation has been taken, take a "negative approach" and investigate the stamp in a manner another person buying it from you might investigate it. The "other buyer" will not give you the benefit of the doubt, so do likewise in your "negative evaluation." Once you have done both positive and negative evaluations of the stamp, combine both figures to get a "net total." *E.G.:* 2.00 positive points (+) and 1.35 negative points (−) = .65 positive points net total.

Then take the standard catalogue value at the present time and multiply the "average catalogue value" by the "net total" to receive the actual cash value. If you have a catalogue that is six months old, add the necessary inflation rate to the old catalogue price before multiplying the price by the "net total."

Once the points have all been added or subtracted, the balance is multiplied with the present catalogue value to determine the "cash" value of the stamp.

To illustrate this formula, let us consider the following stamp in *Scott's Specialized Catalogue of United States Stamps* for 1979: Description- #245, mint, VF, triv. th, OG, NH:

Centering Points=VF   = + 1.00
Positive Points =OG   =⎫
Positive Points =NH   =⎬ + 1.00
Negative Points =1mm th= − .15

Total   + 1.85 × Scott
Value ($1,650.00)

Cash Value = $1,650.00
× 1.85
$3,052.50

If #245 Mint is: F, sc, re-gum NH, th, then the cash value would be:

Centering Points=F   = + .50
Positive Points =re-gum NH= + .10
Negative Points =1 mm th = − .15
Negative Points =1 mm sc = − .20

Total + .25 × Scott
Value
($1,650.00)

Cash Value = $1,650.00
× .25
$412.50

If #245 Mint is: XF, NH, OG, bright color, all perfs intact, *gem! Original Post Office Condition!* Then the cash value would be:

Centering Points=XF   =   2.00
Positive Points =NH   =⎫
Positive Points =OG   =⎬ 1.00
Positive Points =No th = + .00
Positive Points =No sc = + .00

Positive Points = No se   = + .00
Positive Points = perfs intact = + .25
Positive Points = Bright color = + .50
                                _____
Negative Points = Total   = + 3.75 × Scott
                                Value ($1,650.00)

   (None!)

                  Cash Value = $1,650.00
                             × 3.75
                             _____
                             $6,187.50

As you can see from these three illustrations, the cash value can range from approximately $400 to $3,050 to $6,185+ +. With a plus (+) or minus (−) of 10%, you can at least get a ballpark figure of a stamp in relationship to its catalogue value and make more than an "educated guess" when appraising the value and how badly you want to buy it. If you can get a stamp for less than this formula suggests, then you can be safe in your investments, but if the cost is a great deal larger than the formula, perhaps you should re-evaluate the stamps and look at market values more critically. Remember, you will develop a feel for the purchase of stamps as you gather your investments. But do not overpay for a stamp. It is better to pass up a possible bargain and sleep well than to stay awake at night and "curse the darkness." There will always be material for investment, as stamps are constantly being brought to market and the availability is great. So be patient and wait for the "good deals."

THE TRIKILIS INDEX TEST

The following examples are given as a test to enable the reader to try the index and compare his answers to the author's answers. Remember, if your answers are plus (+) or minus (−) 5% (.05), you are safe in your evaluations. If you are a great deal higher, read the section on the Index again.

EXAMPLE I: *#245, F-VF, OG, HR, 1 sp, 1mm vert. cr = ?%

EXAMPLE II: 0#292, VG, H canc., 1 mm th = ?%

EXAMPLE III: *#299, VF, OG, NH, "Post Office Fresh" = ?%

EXAMPLE IV: 0#241, G, L canc, slightly faded, 1 mm sc = ?%

EXAMPLE V: *#244, XF, RG, HR, good color = ?%

EXAMPLE VI: 0#C-13, F, OG, NGS, NH = ?%

EXAMPLE VII: *#122, VF, NG, crisp and bright color, unusual centering for this issue = ?%

ANSWERS TO TRIKILIS INDEX TEST

EXAMPLE I: * = Mint; Scott #245:

F-VF =	+ .75	1 sp =	−.15
OG, HR =	+ .05	1 mm cr =	−.10
	+ .80 +		−.25 = +.55 (answer) (55%)

EXAMPLE II: 0 = used; Scott #292:

VG =	+.25	H canc. =	−.25
		1 mm th =	−.15
	+.25 +		−.40 = −.15 (answer)
			(−15%)
			Space Filler!

EXAMPLE III: *=Mint; Scott #299:

VF =	+1.00	
OG, NH =	+1.00	
color =	+ .50	("Post Office Fresh")
	+ 2.50	(answer, +250%)

EXAMPLE IV: $0=$ used; Scott #241:

G = + .08	slightly faded	= −.15
L canc = + .15	1 mm sc	= −.20
+ .23 +		−.35 = −.12 (answer)

$$-12\%$$
Space Filler!

EXAMPLE V: * $=$ Mint; Scott #244:

XF = +2.00	RG, HR = − .10
good color = + .15	
+ 2.15 +	−.10 = 2.05 (answer)

$$+205\%$$

EXAMPLE VI: $0=$ used; Scott #C-13 (C represents Air Mail Issue):

F	=	+ .50
OG, NGS, NH	=	+ .65
		+ 1.15 (answer) +115%

EXAMPLE VII: * $=$ Mint; Scott #122:

VF = +1.00	NG (No Gum) = −.50
Bright	
Crisp = + .50	
Color	
+1.50	+ −.50 = 1.00 (answer)

$$100\%$$

Special Note: As centering for this issue was noted as above-average for this issue, you may add 10% to 20% to the answer if the stamp is without major faults, and a photograph or visual inspection confirms this.

CARING FOR
AND PROTECTING
YOUR STAMP
COLLECTION

H *ow should I keep my stamps?*
I do not recommend purchasing a stamp album. It is too easy to fall into a collecting habit. Stamps have a "hypnotic effect." The pleasure of obtaining rare and valuable material will cause a "hoarding" feeling to gradually infest your mind. You must refrain from the collecting habit, or valuable dollars will go into the beautiful, aesthetic (non-investment) stamps. It will start only as a manner to display your finds among the less valuable, more common material.

Many dealers will get you started in this manner only to get the collecting bug started in your heart. I personally do not think that anything can beat the pride one receives from acquiring a dozen $1-value Columbian mint stamps (Scott #241). I never tire of looking at six or so $2 Trans-Mississippi stamps. This becomes an obsession, also, but the obsession is to buy more of the same issues at better market prices. You know that they are climbing in value, and you want to have them in your possession before their prices climb out of sight.

I keep rare investment material in a high-quality

stamp stock book. I try to categorize them by issue
and face value. Each stamp is placed in a Hawid
mount (a plastic holder that is sealed at its bottom)
so that the handling of the valuable stamp will be
easier and there will be less risk of damaging the
stamp as it is removed from the book for occasional
inspection.

All stamps kept in safety deposit boxes in books
between Hawid mounts should occasionally be tak-
en out and inspected, because the humidity of a
vault is not often good for prolonged storage.
Stamps must "breathe" or they will eventually
"stick" to their mounts or their books.

When inspection of stamps occurs, do it carefully
and gently so as not to tear the stamps or damage
them accidentally by creasing them. Too often, we
are "bulls in a china shop," and nothing is more
heartbreaking or demoralizing than damaging a
prize rare stamp. You can lose $1,000 in the mere
wink of an eye. *So be very careful!*

Does homeowner's insurance generally cover loss of stamps?

The way most people find out how good their insurance coverage is the hard way. It comes at a time
when they normally need it. Don't be foolish when
dealing with your stamps! Treat them as if each one
were a $100-bill or a new Cadillac. Know your cov-
erage before you make heavy transactions within
the marketplace. If it is necessary, get special coverage to insure your holdings while they are out of the
safety deposit box.

Most homeowner policies only cover stamps under their "Acts of Peril," and only for a maximum of
$500. The Acts of Peril are listed within the policy,
and accidental losses not listed will not be covered
by the policy.

If your dog happens to eat them by accident or an

envelope filled with valuable stamps is accidentally thrown away, you are out the cost of the stamps. The policy will not even pay the $500 in the listed personal-property section. Remember, a major pitfall in dealing with stamps is their fragile condition. The weight of a rare stamp is several times worth that of gold! Sometimes an absent mind can cause you to misplace stamps and totally forget where you put them. Your spouse may accidentally throw "the baby out with the bathwater," so always *place your stamps in a secure place, and never deviate from the habit!*

Where can I obtain insurance coverage for stamps?

When you join the Society for Philatelic Americans, you will receive the opportunity to have insurance rates after one full year of membership. For additional information, you may write to:

Sidney Springer
5480 Wisconsin Avenue, Suite 207
Chevy Chase, Maryland 20015

Should I keep accurate records of my stamp purchases?

The more accurate your records are, the better it will be to know your margin of profit and the percentage of return on your investment. When you buy stocks, you know the purchase price and the commission you paid to receive the stocks.

When you buy stamps, you must also record the amount you paid for the stamps and the commission paid. Both added together will give you the gross payment (excluding any insurance costs and mailing costs) for the lots that you have received.

In the event of your death, any heirs will pay on the cost of stamps to you, and not on the entire value of the appreciated material at time of probate.

This can be very important especially if no records were kept. The stamps might be "net-worthed" by the I.R.S., and then unnecessary payments would result.

Each person should develop a code to show the cost of goods on each lot. Each lot should be kept in separate envelopes or compartments, and corresponding values of their cost should be attached to the compartments for references in case you wish to sell stamps at a later date.

One simple example is to prepare your own cipher de-coder card with corresponding information.

Companies You Buy From (Names)	Code Letter or Number
Company #1	A
Company #2	B
Company #3	C
Company #4	D
Company #5	E
Months—January	7
February	4
March	9
April	11
May	2
Dollars Paid—Numeral 1	b
Numeral 2	z
Numeral 3	m
Numeral 4	p
Numeral 5	r
Numeral 6	a
Numeral 7	c
Numeral 8	k
Numeral 9	x
Numeral 0	y

By assigning each month and numeral a "special" code number, and the continuation of a random listing of vendors you purchase from, it is nearly impossible for anyone not having your code card to figure out what, when, from whom, and what you actually paid for an item. Following is an example:

		From Whom You Purchased		Date		Amount Paid
C/280/zkx	=	Company #3	/	May 1980	/	$289
E/1180/wyyr	=	Company #5	/	April 1980	/	$9,005

There are many ways to read a code, and each person should utilize that which makes him comfortable. It should be simple, easy to use—and, above all, easy to read and understand.

RARE-STAMP
STORIES

There are many stories about people who have found rare stamps, and almost always (if not always) it was totally by accident. No one, unless he is a close relative or lifetime friend, will knowingly take something of great wealth and give it to you. When stamps were first printed, many people handling them in the minting plants were not aware of the importance of their jobs. But early stamp manufacturing was not as closely monitored as it is today. When an error was made, instead of the mistakes being thrown out, many often went out with the regular copies. Not all of them did, for they were destroyed when first found, but some slipped through.

These stamps that slipped through are the ones with which we are concerned here. There are stories of large companies giving presumed worthless papers to their employees for their collecting interests. These papers were later to be found with rarities worth many times what the employees might make in the next ten years.

There are also stories of construction workers tearing down old houses and finding letters between the walls that were later valued at many thousands of dollars. I am sure that we have all heard one unusual stamp story or another. But the three most

famous stamp stories that I enjoy are: the most valuable stamp in the world, the British Guiana of 1856;
the Mauritius Stamp of 1847; and the Inverted C-3
airplane issue of 1918.

THE BRITISH GUIANA OF 1856

In 1856, the postal supply of British Guiana had
been totally used up. The stamps that were due in
from England to replenish the post office had not
yet arrived. So the local postmaster decided to issue
some of his own in order to keep the community sat-
isfied and the mails flowing. Going to a local newspaper, the postmaster used regular printer's type
and the newspaper's press to print the badly needed
postage. Before many of the local issue could be sold
and used by the people of British Guiana, the postage stamps from the Mother Country arrived, and
the supply of locals was destroyed by the postmaster.

No one knows exactly how many of the local British Guiana stamps might have been used. It is impossible to even estimate. But the fact is quite
certain that the tiny stamp must have been produced in more than one copy because it was minted
on a press. And apparently, the press must have
done it more than one up (a single at one time only).

As it happened, approximately twenty years later a young man in England was searching for stamps among old letters and came upon the "black-on-magenta" stamp of British Guiana (1856). It was not a very lovely stamp, especially for a young man "collecting" stamps and wishing to fill his album with colorful material. The corners were "missing" and the condition was not very good. Imagine finding a new stamp that you have never seen before. You do not have a catalogue of the stamp history, since it is too new a hobby for any company to print and sell in great quantity to collectors, who are so totally independent. Therefore, you do not know if a million more of your find exist. If you have an opportunity to sell your find for $1.50 (remember, it is 1876, approximately) and $1.50 buys a great deal more then than it would today, would you have not sold it and perhaps thought then that other stamps like the one you found existed? Most certainly you would have, especially since it is a hobby, and one "ugly" stamp more or less would not be important to you. There is no market for rare stamps, so you would have really lost nothing, and the $1.50 would be better than a poorly colored stamp from an old attic.

After a few more years, the buyer of the stamp sold the entire collection through or to a dealer in Glasgow, Scotland. The entire collection went for approximately $600. The dealer then broke up the collection and sold it to other collectors in bits and pieces. The British Guiana of 1856 was sold to an Austrian Count by the name of Ferrary.

Count Ferrary purchased the stamp for $750 and added it to his collection in Paris, France. The Count was considered eccentric. For who but an eccentric would purchase an ugly stamp for what was at the time a small fortune? Consider investing $750 in 1876 at a simple interest rate of 6% per year:

your investment one hundred years later would be worth $768,000!

The stamp remained part of Count Ferrary's collection for approximately forty years. It was not until the Count's death in 1917 that the stamp was again to be circulated in the stamp world. The Count, being an alien in France, had willed his entire collection to the Berlin Postal Museum in Berlin, Germany. At the time World War I was still being fought, the property of Count Ferrary was confiscated by the French Government. All was to be sold at auction by the French Government, and the proceeds were to be applied to Germany's bill for "reparations."

The entire collection was sold in a series of fourteen large auctions that were held in Paris between 1921 and 1925. The collection brought more than $2,000,000 which was applied to the reparation of Germany.

At one of the auctions held by the French Government, an American millionaire, Arthur Hind, purchased the stamp for $32,500 plus a government tax. The total amount exceeded $38,000 which, prior to the "crash" and the Great Depression, was a great deal of money.

The stamp had a Scott catalogue value in 1929 of $32,500, even though the tax had placed the cash paid for the stamp over $38,000. This is an early illustration of how the actual cash value was greater than the catalogue value.

A short time before Mr. Hind's death in 1933, he gave the stamp to his wife. Mrs. Hind placed the stamp in her bank's vault, where it remained for seven years. The catalogue value had risen to $50,000.

In 1940, Mr. Frederick Small, wishing to remain anonymous, purchased it privately for more than $40,000. It was not much of an increase from the money paid fifteen years earlier by Mr. Hind.

In 1970, the stamp was sold for more than $280,000 at auction, making it the most money ever paid for one stamp. It was purchased by Irwin Weinberg, a Wilkes Barre, Pennsylvania, stamp dealer. He acted on behalf of a nine-member syndicate agreeing to hold the stamp for ten years before trying to sell it.

On April 5, 1980, the stamp was brought to auction in the Robert A. Siegel's Rarities Auction at the Waldorf-Astoria Hotel in New York City. Several buyers and spectators were present for this historical philatelic event, which lasted less than one minute. When the gavel finally banged, marking the end of the 1¢ British Guiana rarity sale, the buyer paid $850,000 plus the 10% buyer's commission. This made the total amount paid for a single stamp $935,000!

This was not the million-dollar sale that everyone in the philatelic world said that it would be, but Mr. Weinberg and his associates were certainly not complaining!

THE MAURITIUS STAMP OF 1847

You have probably heard the expression, "Haste makes waste." In most cases, I am sure that there is a great deal of truth in this proverb, but there is an instance where "haste created a fortune" in philatelic material.

In 1847, postage stamps had been in use for only a very short period of time. The concept was so new that it had not even been introduced to the postal authorities of the island of Mauritius. Mauritius, a British-owned island located in the Indian Ocean, was governed by a person recently appointed to office. As postage stamps were recently invented for postal use, the new governor's wife wished to use them on her invitations to the inaugural ball.

Commissioning a local jeweler to engrave the island's first plates, the jeweler was placed under great pressure to produce the plates for immediate usage. Working late into the night without experience and being rushed by the governor's wife, the engraver made a serious mistake not noted until the proofing of the first few sheets. The jeweler erroneously engraved the words "Post Office" instead of the words "Post Paid" upon the stamp.

When the error was discovered, the governor's wife would not be delayed even one day. She took enough of the stamps to mail her invitations, and the rest of the errors were destroyed. How many were used cannot really be estimated, because no one really knows exactly how many invitations were sent out. There were two values issued in this first printing of the error—a 1¢ orange, and a 2¢ blue. There are approximately thirty stamps known to be in existence. All have been accidentally discovered. Both mint and used copies have made it into the stamp world. In 1929, the catalogue value of the Scott #1, Imperforate 1¢ orange, was $20,000 for a mint issue; and the Scott #2, Imperforate 2¢ blue, was $17,000 for mint. The #1 was $12,500 for a used copy, and the #2 was $15,000.

In the 1981 catalogue, the stamps have grown so greatly in value that one is tempted to search every nook and cranny to find one. The #1 mint is now the same price as the #2 mint, and used catalogue values are also identical. The #1 and #2 mint are catalogued at $400,000, and their used values are $250,000! This is a considerable amount for a hasty mistake made more than one hundred thirty years ago.

THE "UPSIDE-DOWN AIRPLANE OF 1918"

There are hundreds of stories about printing errors: some deliberate and known prior to release of the issue, as in the case of the Mauritius stamp; and some stories of mistakes made without the knowledge of the postal authorities until "the horse was out of the barn," and it was too late to close the door. The most interesting one to me is the United States first air mail issue of 1918.

I think that this airplane stamp story is of more interest to me because it happened in the United States not in the mid-1800s, as in other countries, but because it happened just after the turn of the century, when our post office was initiating air transportation of mail and elected to print three issues for their services. A one-color 6¢ issue, (C-1, orange only), a one-color 16¢ issue (C-2, green only), and a two-color issue for the 24¢ (red and blue, C-3) were the first three stamps issued for this purpose.

Of the three denominations, the 24¢ issue was the first to be released by the post office, as the air mail rate was fixed on May 15, 1918, at 24¢ per ounce, or a fraction thereof, which included special-delivery service. The first service was between Washington, D.C., Philadelphia, and New York. Letters and sealed parcels could be mailed at any of the three cities and sent to any city in the United States or its possessions.

The stamps were first placed on sale on May 13, 1918, in Washington, D.C. On May 14, 1918, Mr. W. J. Robey went to the New York Avenue branch of the post office located at 1317 New York Avenue, N.W., in Washington, D.C., to purchase a sheet of the new 24¢ air mail issue for his stamp collection. Because of poor centering of those sheets available, Mr. Robey declined buying them and was told by the clerk that a new shipment from the mint was due to arrive before closing time. Mr. Robey returned at noon just as the stamps had arrived. Asking the clerk if he might have a sheet of the new 24¢ issue, the clerk reached under the counter, handing the inverted 24¢ air mail sheet to Mr. Robey. Mr. Robey's heart must have stopped for a moment as he viewed his "find." He promptly paid the clerk and immediately asked if he had any more sheets available. The clerk handed him the rest for his inspection, but all were normal and obviously did not interest Mr. Robey. He then showed the clerk what he had purchased, and the clerk rushed to the telephone to tell the mint what had happened. Mr. Robey immediately left the post office with his find in hand.

Mr. Robey telegrammed Mr. Percy Mann, of Philadelphia, Pennsylvania, the editor of *Mekeel's Weekly*, a philatelic periodical. He advised Mr. Mann of his find and requested him to announce it in his next column.

Immediately the next day, Mr. Mann was in Washington, D.C., to view the sheet. Upon his confirmation that the sheet in fact existed, he offered Mr. Robey $10,000 for the sheet of inverted airplanes. Mr. Robey declined the offer because he was well aware of what the open market would bring for his prize. So Mr. Robey went to New York City to see if his sheet would be of interest to the philatelic community there. He returned to Philadelphia to Mr. Mann after he had received offers ranging from $250 to $2,500 for the sheet.

Mr. Mann took Mr. Robey to see another stamp collector, Mr. Eugene Klein of Philadelphia. After viewing the sheet, Mr. Klein asked Mr. Robey what he would like to receive for the inverted sheet. Mr. Robey replied that he would have to have $15,000 for his sheet of stamps. Within a few days, Mr. Klein paid Mr. Robey the $15,000 he had requested for his sheet. He had made $14,976 profit on his $24 investment in less than one week!

The sheet contained 100 stamps at 24¢ each (amount charged by the post office for postage). They were sold for $150 each to Mr. Klein less than a week later. He had no idea if the other three sheets were in the market at the time. Remember, this was only one-quarter of the printed full sheet. If the first quarter made it through inspection, then it was quite possible for the other three sheets of 100 to also be in existence.

Today, only the Robey sheet is known to be in existence. The clerk alerted the main minting office and the other three sheets were probably located and destroyed. A postal employee is required by law to surrender to his supervisors any and all defects discovered either in the mint or at the post office level.

On May 25, Mr. Klein offered to sell portions of the sheet for $175 for straight-edge copies and $250 for regular copies. On June 1, he announced that he had sold the entire sheet for an undisclosed amount to Col. E. H. R. Green.

It was Col. Green's desire to retain certain parts of the sheet for his own personal collection. He placed the balance with a dealer for dispersal into the philatelic world. The prices for the liquidation of the balance were given only "upon request."

I do not know the breakdown for each of the units sold, but I can assume that there are many individual stamps in the world today. Some are regular and some are with a straight edge. The plate block is probably in existence. It would be the unique part of the sheet. I know that a block of four was held by Princeton University and sold by Harmers of New York on June 8, 1976. It was valued at the time at $200,000. It was being sold to build a wing on the Firestone Library at Princeton University. There are presumably only three such blocks in existence.

A single stamp was recently sold by Jacques C. Schiff, Jr., Inc., of Ridgefield Park, New Jersey. It was in their September 22–24, 1978, auction held in Indianapolis, Indiana, for the A.P.S. Stamp Convention. The stamp sold for $62,500. It was Very Fine centering, with a hinge remnant, faintly thin, and with a tiny natural paper speck. The Scott 1979 catalogue valued it at $65,000, thus making the entire sheet of Robey's inverts worth $6,500,000! (That is, if one were to buy the three blocks and the plate block at the single piece price!)

PHILATELIC RARITIES AND PRICES REALIZED

July, 1979–June 30, 1980

Block of Four, C-3 Invert (Mint) "Princeton Block" Upside-Down Airplane — $500,000 (plus $50,000 commission)

Canada 1959 Block of Four (Mint) 5¢ Seaway Invert — $70,000 (plus $7,000 commission)

Canal Zone Thatcher Ferry Bridge Error 1962 (Mint) Silver Bridge Omitted — $55,000 (sold at private treaty)

U.S. 1869 Pictorial Scott #121b 30¢ Blue & Carmine Invert (Used) — $70,000 (plus $7,000 commission)

U.S. Bank Note Special Printing Scott #167–177 (Mint) Complete Set — $75,000 (plus $7,500 commission)

U.S. Columbian $4 Block of Four (Mint) Bottom Right Corner Margin Block with "CC" Letters on Salvage — $57,500 (plus $5,750 commission)

U.S. Pan-American 1¢ (Mint) Center Inverted Scott #294a — $11,500 (plus $1,500 commission)

U.S. Pan-American 1¢ Scott #294a Strip of — $55,000 (plus $5,500 commission)

4 with Imprint &
Plate Number Cen-
ters Inverted (Mint)

U.S. Pan-American 2¢ Center Inverted (Mint) Scott #295a	$40,000 (plus $4,000 commission)
U.S. Pan-American 4¢ (Mint) Center Invert-ed Scott #296a	$10,500 (plus $1,050 commission)
U.S. Blue Imperforate Block of 81 (Mint) Scott #315 Including Two Imprint & Plate Blocks of Six	$57,000 (plus $5,700 commission)
U.S. Air Mail Invert (Mint) Scott #C-3a	$125,000 (plus $12,500 commission)
U.S. Zepps Small Die Proofs Scott #C13P–C15p (believed to be only two sets known)	$32,500 (plus $3,250 commission)
U.S. Zepps Plate Blocks of Six Scott #C13–C15 (Mint)	$55,000 (plus $5,500 commission)
Canal Zone Thatcher 4¢ 1962 Plate Block of Ten (Mint) Silver Bridge Omitted	$130,000 (plus $13,000 commission)
Bermuda, 1854, 1¢ Red on Bluish "Perot" Provisional (X2) on Folded Letter to St. Georges (only two known)	$210,000 (plus $21,000 commission)

British Guiana, 1856, 1¢ Black on Magenta (13). Rarest stamp in the world! Only one in existence!	$850,000 (plus $85,000 commission)
Canada, 1959 5¢ Seaway Invert Scott #387a (Mint)	$19,000 (plus $1,900 commission)
Greece, 1861, 20L Blue on Bluish Bottom Right Corner Margin; Block of 25 with Full Imprint at Bottom (Mint #4)	$52,500 (plus $5,250 commission)
Mauritius, 1848, 2p Dark Blue "Penoe" Error, Earliest Impression Scott #4d	$60,000 (plus $6,000 commission)

THE GREAT AMERICAN RIP-OFF

This United States 1¢ stamp was minted in 1925; in 1978, a dealer had no better use for it than to affix it to a letter—as 1¢ postage.

Many of you have always heard that there is great potential, as far as investments are concerned, in collecting new issues of United States postage stamps in plate-block form. There is no greater myth in existence than this myth, which was created by our own government.

The United States has started this myth to create a new method in minting money. The United States post office generally prints from 50,000,000 to 150,000,000 of any new commemorative at the present time. I would go so far to say that the average minting of a stamp today is 150,000,000. Therefore, the chances of these stamps gaining any value is practically nil. If you will compare the value of a commemorative minted in 1935 (Scott catalogue #758), which was printed in a quantity of 2,168,088, you will note in the Scott 1981 catalogue that the value is $0.75. In forty-three years, the three-cent value has risen to twenty-five times its face value.

But, if you read *Linn's Stamp Newspaper,* you will see dealers offering only 85% to 90% of face value for similar stamps. This means that a $100 investment in 1935 would be worth only $90 today. But what is the buying power of that $90 today, as compared to the buying power of the $100 in 1935?

This has become such a big business for the post office that philatelic centers are being opened up right in the post office buildings throughout the United States. Yes, these are retail stores operating for a profit. It is estimated that there are approximately 20,000,000 stamp collectors in the United States alone. These people are collecting stamps as a hobby, and only a very small percentage of them are serious stamp investors. The post office mints more stamps then are needed to carry the mails today. Approximately 25% of all stamps minted wind up in the stamp dealer's vaults or the stamp collector's stamp books.

This would mean that the American citizen spends $250,000,000 per year for stamps for collecting. The government exchanges little pieces of brightly colored paper for large American greenbacks and skims $250,000,000 out of the economy each year. Yes, it is a new method of minting a different kind of money. Yet, inflation will pound the hell out of it before it gets half a chance to be used.

I hate to think how much money is being held in

stamp albums or safety deposit boxes by hobbyists.

If, on the other hand, you would have invested the $100 in Scott catalogue #245 in 1935, you could have purchased five copies from a stamp dealer. If they were only Fine quality stamps, today the Scott catalogue value would be in excess of $9,000, with an average increase in the last five years of 22% per year!

Do not be duped into becoming another foolish American stamp collector. Do not buy new stamp issues!

Naturally, there is always an exception to the rule. The exception here would be to look for stamp errors. But, remember, most post office employees are stamp collectors, and they get first crack at any errors that might slip past the inspector's eye. But keep looking; you might get lucky.

APPENDIX I

U.S. STAMPS OF INTEREST TO THE INVESTOR,
with Identification for Centering and Visual Condition

⊙ #2, G, L canc.

⊙ #1, with grid canc. L

✱ #118, F-VF, sp LR
corner

✱ #120, F, several sp

✱ #122, F-VF, few sp

⊙ #122, VG, few sp

✳ #241, F-VF

✳ #242, F-VF

✳ #243, F-VF, sharp
impression

✳ #244, VG-F, few sp

U.S. STAMPS FOR THE INVESTOR

* #245, F-VF

* #292, VF

* #294a. VG, invert

* #296a, VG-F, invert

* Block/4 C3a, invert,
extremely rare
Princeton block

* C3a. F-VF, invert   * C3

* C13, VF, Zepp

* C14, VF, Zepp

* C15, F-VF, Zepp

APPENDIX II

MISCELLANEOUS RARITIES AND CURIOSITIES

#303, mint, 1902 issue, #5 Marshall. Courtesy of Robert A. Siegel.

#314a, used, imperf, wavy line machine cancel, Schermack Ty III private perforations. Rare. Courtesy of Robert A. Siegel.

#317, mint, vertical coil pair. Courtesy of Robert A. Siegel.

#245, mint, $5 Columbian issue. Courtesy of Robert A. Siegel.

#118a, mint, without grill, pictorial issue of 1869. Courtesy of Robert A. Siegel.

#12, mint, imperf. Courtesy of Robert A. Siegel.

#C3a, carmine, rose and blue, center inverted. Courtesy Robert A. Siegel.

#10 × 1, mint, single, postmaster's provisional. Courtesy of H. R. Harmer.

#10 × 1 and 10 × 2, mint (10 × 2a) se-tenant with 5¢. Courtesy of H. R. Harmer.

#10 × 1 - 10 × 2, complete sheet, postmaster's provisional, Providence, R. I., Welcome B. Sales, Postmaster. Courtesy of H. R. Harmer.

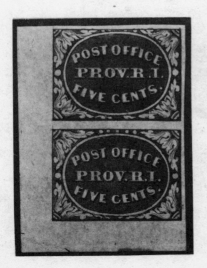

#10 × 1, postmaster's provisional, mint, vertical pair. Courtesy of H. R. Harmer.

#4, mint, re-issue,
block of four. Courtesy
of H. R. Harmer.

#3, mint, re-issue,
block of four. Courtesy
of H. R. Harmer.

#387a, Canadian
invert, mint, rare late-
twentieth-century
error. Courtesy of
Robert A. Siegel.

#1, mint, block of
eight, very rare.
Courtesy of H. R.
Harmer.

#1, used, block of
four, very rare.
Courtesy of H. R.
Harmer.

#1, mint, vertical
strip of three, rare.
Courtesy of H. R.
Harmer.

#1, mint, horizontal
pair. Courtesy of H. R.
Harmer.

#2a, used on cover,
diagonal half as "5¢"
postage instead of
"whole stamp" face
value of 10¢. Courtesy
of H. R. Harmer.

#2a, used on cover,
diagonal half as "5¢"
postage instead of
"whole stamp" face
value of 10¢. Courtesy
of H. R. Harmer.

#1, used, separated
pair on cover.
Courtesy of H. R.
Harmer.

#2, used, on cover.
Courtesy of H. R.
Harmer.

#2, used, four single
stamps on cover.
Courtesy of H. R.
Harmer.

#2, used, bottom
margin stamp on
cover. Courtesy of
H. R. Harmer.

#1, mint, block of
nine, very rare.
Courtesy of H. R.
Harmer.

#1, mint, horizontal
block of six, very rare.
Courtesy of H. R.
Harmer.

ONE SET SPECIMEN POSTAGE STAMPS,

ISSUE OF 1869.

Denominations—1, 2, 3, 6, 10, 12, 15, 24, 30, and 90 cents.   Value, $1.93.

#123–132, pictorial
re-issue set. Courtesy
of H. R. Harmer.

#292, imprint block
of ten, very rare
indeed. Courtesy of
Harmers of New York.

APPENDIX III

PHILATELIC GLOSSARY

Accessories—Tools or instruments utilized by philatelists in examining and classifying stamps—e.g., tongs (tweezers), watermark defectors, perforation guage, stamp mounts, hinges, magnifying glass, etc.

Acknowledgement-of-Receipt Stamp—Stamp specifically issued to pay the fee for notification by the post office that your letter or parcel has been delivered to the addressee.

Address—Indicating to whom the cover or folded envelope was sent.

Adhesive—The "gum" on the back of a mint stamp that will affix the stamp to the article when moistened and applied with slight pressure.

Aerophilately—That area of philatelic interest which deals in air mail stamps, air mail covers, or first-flight covers.

Air Mail Stamps—Stamps specifically issued for matter being sent by air.

Albino—A die impression on a stamped envelope where the ink has not been applied, but the impression often exists.

Appearance—The physical condition of the article or stamp.

Approvals—Stamps submitted (usually via the mail) for your inspection and possible purchase; unpurchased stamps would be returned to the seller by the buyer, with payment generally enclosed.

Army Official Stamps—Stamps issued to army officials for use in correspondence for "official" or government business. Now obsolete, official business is now franked without stamps, but with the presence of official franking.

Arrow Block—A block of stamps on whose margin is printed an arrow with a thin line following up the center in the path of the perforations; used by the printer to register color or as a guide for perforation. Sheets may have from two to four "arrows," depending upon the particular issue.

Artist's Initials—The initials of the artist or engraver can be found directly under each stamp or in the margin of the sheet.

Auction—A public or private offering of stamps or collections in which one either acquires or disposes of material. Lots are generally sold to the highest floor bidder, unless a bid received by mail is greater. Commission paid to the auctioneer is generally given by the person disposing of the material. A good way to liquidate, but often major auction houses take 20% of the gross as their share for the sale. Commission is often negotiable. There may also be a "lotting fee."

Backstamp—A postmark stamped on the back of a piece of incoming mail to show time and date of receipt by the post office of addressee. This is an important mark on first-flight covers, verifying the article was carried from one point to another via a certain route.

Balloon Posts—Mail carried by balloon.

Bank Mixture—Stamps acquired from bank house's incoming mail; generally a mixture and sold by the pound.

Banknote Issues—Stamps printed for federal post office by three companies from 1870 to 1887. The three Companies were: American Banknote Company, Continental Banknote Company, and National Banknote Company.

Bicentennial—Two-hundredth-year anniversary of a "special event" generally celebrated or "commemorated" by an issue illustrating that event. For example, in 1932, the U.S. Post Office issued a stamp to celebrate the birth year of George Washington, 1732. (See Scott catalogue #704–715.)

Bicolor—A two-color stamp. (*See* Scott catalogue # 120, 121, 122, 294–299, 547, 573, etc.)

Bisect—Portion of a stamp generally used to pay postage on a piece where the post office has depleted its stock of a smaller issue. Stamp can be bisected in half to represent one-half of face value of issue—e.g., a 10¢ issue cut in half would be used as two 5¢ issues.

Black Jacks—Name given to U.S. 2¢ black issue of Andrew Jackson (1862 Scott catalogue #73), designed by J. W. Dodge.

Block—Generally means 4 unseparated stamps in a "block" or rectangular shape, 2 stamps high and 2 stamps wide; usually listed as block of 4, block of 6, block of 8, etc.

Boardwalk Margin—Very wide (almost oversized) paper margins around the 4 sides of a stamp between the frameline of the design of the stamp and the stamp's edge.

Bogus—Counterfeit or fake; imitation of a stamp.

Booklet—Complete small packet of stamps consisting generally of 2 or more vertical blocks of 6 stamps. Each block is perforated vertically through the center; each pane is perforated horizontally on all inside edges, and all outside edges are straight edges.

Booklet Pane—A block of stamps, usually 6, forming a page stapled into a booklet.

Border—A stamp's edge or frame around its design (generally not part of design).

Bottom—The lower edge of the article indicated.

Bourse—A marketplace where philatelic material and supplies can be bought or sold; stamps can often be traded and exchanged.

Bull's-Eye Cancellation—A postmark placed directly on the center of a stamp or a block of stamps showing city, state, and date of cancellation.

Bureau Precancels—The Bureau of Printing and Engraving in Washington, D.C., pre-cancellation of stamps. (*See* Precancel.)

Burels or Burelage—To discourage counterfeiting of stamps, a fine overall network of dots or lines is printed on the surface of stamps, in addition to the design of the stamps.

Cachet—A rubber stamp, printed, or engraved impression on an envelope which describes the occasion for which the envelope was mailed. Uses for cachets are numerous: space events, naval events, first-day issues, first flights, medical discoveries, etc.

Canceled to Order—Postage stamps canceled without ever being used; done extensively in Europe, to offer both dealers and collectors mint and used new issues (very rarely an investment area in new issues).

Cancellation—A defacing method employed by the postal authorities to show that the stamp has been used, and usually it is done with an ink that cannot be removed without damaging the stamp. Cancellation can show city, state, and date; or it can be just an ink spot. Older issues were often blue, orange, red, brown, and other colors. Some colors are more difficult to find; hence, they are often listed as being more expensive in the catalogue.

Carrier Stamps—In earlier times, some mail was delivered by private companies from the post office to the addressee. Special stamps were used by postal and private organizations to distinguish the difference. First delivery of mail by our post office was from one post office to another without charge to addressee or sender. Mail had to be picked up at the post office by the addressee, as there was no delivery to their homes.

Catalogue—Organized listing of stamps compiled by an authoritative source well versed in that specific topical area in which pertinent information is given and a relative value is established by the fair-market value of that particular issue.

Catalogue Value—Several publishers recognized by dealers and collectors create books each year to illustrate the normal market price of an "average" stamp during the past 12 months. Stamps of superior quality and centering are worth two or three times the catalogue value, depending on the popularity or the issue and the number originally minted. Likewise, stamps of poorer quality of an identical popular issue may only be worth a small percentage of the listed catalogue value. Even one publisher may greatly differ in opinion from another in the "average" price of an identical issue.

Centennial—One-hundredth-year anniversary of a "special" event, generally celebrated or "commemorated" by an issue illustrating that event. For example, in 1944, the post office issued a stamp to celebrate the 100th anniversary of the telegraph, 1844, with Scott catalogue # 924.

Centering—The positioning of the stamp's design in relationship to its borders or margins. If it is exactly in the center of the paper with equal margins (borders) on all 4 sides, the stamp is said to be "perfectly centered." May be described also as extremely fine (XF). General centering descriptions are average (A), good (G), very good (VG), fine (F), very fine (VF), extremely fine (XF). On a scale of 1 to 10, with 10 being the finest, the most desirable centering would be as follows:

XF— VF—F—VG— G—A
10+— 8—6— 4— 2—1

Center Line Block—Considered the most valuable block of stamps on a sheet; removed from the sheet where the vertical and horizontal guidelines intersect.

Centimeter—A metric unit of measure.

Charity Stamps—Sometimes called "semi-postals"; sold for greater value than face, the difference going to charity for their work.

Circular Date Stamp—A round printed impression placed on an article showing city, state, and date postage was canceled.

Coil Stamps—Vending or stamp-affixing machine stamps; produced in a roll form which can contain up to 500 or 1,000 stamps of a single denomination. (*See* Horizontal-Coil and Vertical Coil stamps.)

Colored Cancellation—Stamps canceled in any color *but* black.

Commemorative Stamps—Stamps issued to honor a famous person or historical event.

Complete—Having all stamps generally found within the area specified—*e.g.*, complete set; or complete issue for the year 1957; or complete color variety.

Compound Perforations—A stamp that has 2 different perforations, the vertical perforation being different from the horizontal. The 1944 issues, Scott catalogue #922, 923, and 924, were perforated 11 × 10½.

Condition—Refers to "quality" of a stamp. Often determined by centering, gum, brightness of the issue. In a used or canceled stamp, the crispness of the postmark and positioning of it can determine condition. Means the "physical" appearance of the stamp and its relationship to its original post office "condition." Stamps which appear to be "in original post office condition" are of great value!

Control Marks—Marks placed on stamps or in sheet margins by postal authorities for control purposes.

Cordial Stamps—Revenue stamps used on liquor or cordials to pay the tax to the government.

Corner Blocks—A block of stamps with salvage (paper remnants of the sheet) remaining on 2 sides of the block.

Counterfeit—A bogus or imitation of a genuine stamp; generally done of the rare or expensive stamps issued.

Cover—An envelope or part of an envelope.

Crease—Refers to "condition" of the stamp. It's a physical property that can be natural or inflicted by accident. It can often be seen easily, but requires special handling so as not to worsen the condition. It may be a vertical or horizontal score, which, depending on the severity, can cheapen the value of a stamp tremendously!

Cut Square—Postal stationery stamps that are cut from envelopes; early collectors disregarded keeping envelopes intact, and many great values were decreased by this method of collecting.

Dandy Roll—Used for watermarking paper as the paper pulp comes from the vats. Wire rollers with the design impressed upon them bear down upon the paper, giving the finished paper the laid or woven appearance found in many stamps.

Date Stamp—A marking or cancellation indicating the

date a cover, folded envelope, letter, or piece was of-
ficially "stamped."

Definitive—A regular issue of stamps; different from
commemoratives, provisionals, or stamps issued for
temporary use.

Denomination—The face value indicated on the stamp—
e.g., 5¢, 10¢, $1.00, etc.

Department Stamps—Stamps issued for the uses of several departments of "official status"—*e.g.*, War Department, U.S. Post Office Department, Department of
Agriculture, Department of the Navy, or Department
of Justice.

Die—A hand or machine-engraved block of metal from
which printing plates are prepared in order to print
stamps.

Die Proofs—Impression or print of the "die" indicates
what the stamp will look like, a printing proof.

Disturbed—"Having a problem. . . ."—or not displaying a
normal appearance.

Document—Manuscript, record, or writing of some official purpose.

Documentary Stamps—Stamps applied to documents,
bills of lading, mortgages, wills, indicating revenues
issued against same.

Double Circular Date Stamp—Having 2 circular date
stamps.

Double Impressions—Two impressions of the same design on the same stamp.

Double-Line Watermark—Paper bearing a marking within the weaving of its fiber that is visible in watermark
solution having a double line in the creation of the
"hidden image."

Double Transfer—A stamp printed from a design, in error, which was impressed twice by the master dies in
preparation of the plate. Generally, the "double
transfer" appears "out of focus."

Duplicate—To list identical lots, or stamps within a lot, as
in an auction catalogue or mail bid offer.

Early Impression—The first printing of a stamp on a
press, as opposed to a later printing. The first printing

is the sharpest because the plate is new, and the later printing is "fuzzy" because the plate begins to show its wear.

Electric-Eye Perforation—Machines equipped with electronic eyes to guide the perforating pins up the center of the stamp's margins which results in exact perforation for well-centered stamps.

Electro or Electroplate—In printing very large press runs of stamps, a printing plate is made by duplicating the original plate, the original plate always being available for such a purpose.

Embossed—In stamps, it is a raised surface or a low relief in relationship to the surface of the paper; stamped envelopes are generally "embossed" and printed on the surface of the paper of the envelope.

Engrave—To cut or etch into a printing plate for the purpose of printing stamps from these plates; the plate is applied with great pressure to the paper, leaving the ink raised above the surface of the paper. An engraved stamp can be "tested" gently by "rubbing" the edge of a stamp tong over the surface of the stamp and "feeling" the ridges of the ink as it passes.

Engraver's Initials—Engraver's initials appearing in the sheet margin or in smaller letters below the bottom frame line of a stamp's design.

Engraver's Proof—A proof taken from an engraving to show how the stamp will look when completed; helps to keep mistakes from happening in the printing run.

Entire—Meaning the "whole" piece: an "entire" envelope with stamp, postmark, address, letter, etc., just as received by the addressee in the mail.

Envelope—A cover having contained or containing a letter or document.

Envelope Cut Square—On a stamped envelope, the stamp portion cut in a square shape from the envelope; often lessens the value, as the "entire" piece is worth more intact.

Error—A mistake; design of a stamp that has something wrong with it: can be perforation, color, paper, or printing. It can be more valuable unless run is extremely large and error is not caught.

Essay—On a proposed new stamp issue, it is a group of proofs run in color and used for determining the final color or design to be used for the initial press run.

Estimate (est.)—An approximate value.

Estimated Cash Value—Approximate cash market value that the "lot" is expected to realize when sold.

Expertize—To determine the stamp as genuine, an expert or authority will examine it to verify it. Any imperfections which may not be visible to the untrained eye can also be determined.

Face Value—The cash value of a postage stamp as printed in its design.

Facsimile—Often a fake or duplicate not having any intrinsic value; an exact duplication or likeness of a stamp or piece.

Fake—A counterfeit, bogus, or altered stamp made to represent the genuine article. Often, the altered stamp may have a color or perforation change, so as to increase its value.

Farley's Follies—The "Special Printings of 1935" printed during the administration of James A. Farley, Postmaster General of the U.S.A.

First-Day Cover (F.D.C.)—An envelope bearing a newly issued stamp postmarked on the first day of sale at a city designated by the post office department.

First Day Issue (F.D.I.)—The first day a new issue is placed on sale.

First-Flight Cover (F.F.C.)—An envelope carried on a first-flight plane opening a new air mail route. A special cancellation and descriptive cachet usually are affixed to the cover at the point of origin.

Fiscal Cancellation—Used for revenue (rather than normal postal purposes), it is a cancellation on a stamp applied by pen, indelible pencil, or rubber stamp. The value of the stamp can be reduced considerably with this type of cancellation.

Flat Plate—Flatbed press printing of a stamp; process considered slower than curved-plate rotary-press method of printing.

Flown Cover—An envelope (cover) carried by air.

Folded Letter—Letter folded in a fashion in which its back becomes the cover, bearing the stamp and address of its ultimate destination.

Forgery—A counterfeit or bogus stamp made by experts with intent to defraud.

Frame (or Frame Line)—It is the outer printed border of the design on a stamp.

Frank (or Franking)—The official symbol used by government offices to post mail without using postage stamps. Use of this franking symbol for purposes other than government business is a federal crime.

Freak—An error or irregularity in a stamp that separates it from the normal issue because of a part perforation, a special color cancellation, a double print, or an improper registration of a color in a multi-colored stamp (an inverted color).

Fugitive Inks—Some stamps use "special inks" in their production to prevent forgery, virtually making it impossible to re-use the stamp. If washing is tried by the forger, the ink will run off or fade easily.

General Collection—A collection of stamps of the entire world, without respect to specialization in any area.

General Postage—Stamps that are issued for ordinary mail use; not air mail stamps, postage due stamps, parcel post stamps, revenue stamps, etc.

Gravure—Same as "photogravure."

Grill—An "embossing" deliberately placed on a stamp, consisting of a small square of miniature pyramids in parallel rows impressed so as to break the fibers of the paper, allowing the cancellation ink to be more easily absorbed by the stamp, preventing the re-use of it for postage by washing; discontinued after new cancellation inks were discovered by the post office to achieve the same desired results.

Gum—The coating of adhesive (glue) on a stamp used to adhere it to the envelope or article for postage; can be on a mint (unused) or pre-canceled (used) stamp.

Gum Crease (Gum Cr.)—A crease in the gum side only.

Gutter—Generally found on many sheets in the U.S. "Farley's Follies" or "Special Printings of 1935," it is the blank space between the panes of a sheet of stamps.

Handstamp (H/S)—The hand cancellation applied to the postage stamp, usually done by a rubber stamp. (Steel stamps have also been used.) Collectors now use the term for some first-day covers.

Heavy Cancel—Extremely dark cancellation that often smudges visual image of stamp's design; often a large area is affected.

Heavy Hinge Remnant (H.H.R.)—An extra-large piece of a hinge remaining on the back of a stamp, or having more than one hinge remnant on a stamp.

Helio—Same as "heliogravure."

Heliogravure—A type of "photogravure" printing of postage stamps used in the early process of photogravure printing.

Hinge Remnant (H.R.)—A piece of a hinge remaining on the back of a stamp.

Hinges (H)—Small pieces of rectangularly gummed glassine paper used to mount stamps in stamp albums; should never be used on mint stamps with original gum, as it will subtract from the value of the stamps.

Horizontal Coil—A coil stamp that is perforated vertically and has 2 straight edges running horizontally at the top and bottom of the stamp. It often comes on rolls for machine dispensing in post offices or retail outlets selling stamps by machine.

Horizontal Crease (Horz. Cr.)—A crease in a stamp running horizontally to the design.

Horizontal Pair—Two stamps horizontally joined.

Imperforate (Imperf.)—Stamps printed in sheets without perforations; stamps must be cut by a scissors or knife to be separated from the sheet.

Impression—The image left on a printed sheet as taken from the printing press or plate.

Imprint—Markings in the salvage of pane or stamps, indicating bureau responsible for minting that issue.

Imprint Block—A block of stamps, taken from a complete sheet or pane, to which is attached the selvage, bearing in its margin the printer's name or *imprint*.

Incomplete—Not containing all parts or pieces of the items listed between the 2 numbers, but generally having both the numbers indicated—*e.g.*, 45/365 may have numbers 45 through 133, not 134, 135 through 234, not 235 through 265, 266 through 361, not 362, 363 through 365. Generally, high catalogue values are also indicated.

Insured Letter Stamps—Stamps issued as for payment on insured letters by the post office for their insurance fees.

Intaglio—Any type of recessed printing in which the inked image of the plate is below the surface.

Internal Revenue—The federal government's revenue tax collected within the country.

Invert—A multicolor stamp having one of the colors accidentally printed upside down, thereby creating an "error." (*See* Scott catalogue issues of #294a, #296a and #C3a.)

Journal Stamps—Prepayment postage stamps issued for the sole purpose of mailing journals, magazines, newspapers, etc.

Killer—A postmarking device used to obliterate a stamp, making re-use of it impossible. Stamps damaged by this method are more worthless than normal cancellation, unless postmark may be from a rare cancellation.

Last-Day Cancellation (L.D.C.)—The last-day postmark of a post office being closed permanently by the post office department.

Letterpress—Typography (surface printing); printing done from halftones or line plates by ordinary typesetting methods of machinery and printing; stamps are said to have been printed by "letterpress."

Letter Sheet—A stamp printed on a sheet of paper designed so that it may be folded to form an envelope suitable for mailing; air mail letters throughout the world are now popular in this form.

Light Hinge—Mark left on gum of stamp after removal of hinge in which gum remains virtually intact, but not enough to merit "Never Hinge" status.

Line Block—The guidelines found on a sheet of stamps for color registration, perforation, or cutting of the full press-run sheets; line may run horizontally or vertically between rows of stamps; a block with this line is fewer than a block without this line.

Line Pair—Vertical or horizontal pair of stamps through which a line passes on adjoining perforations.

Lithography (Litho)—A printing method used to apply the ink directly on the surface of the paper; the image is photographically printed on the plate, and quality for color reproduction is extremely good.

Local Stamps—Stamps used within a city or district within a country, and solely restricted to that specific geographical area.

Looseleaf Album—A stamp book that has removable pages for adding or deleting without disturbing the binding.

Lotting Fee—Amount charged by auction house, over and above the usual house commission, to a consignee, or individual seller, for listing a stamp or stamps in an auction.

Major Varieties—Major variations of one issue over another issue.

Maltese Cross—A cancellation used by the British during the 1840s; can also be found as a watermark.

Manuscript—Often referring to manuscript cancellation, in which a pen is used to hand-cancel the cover or stamp.

Margin (MGR)—That portion surrounding a sheet of stamps in which the paper is unprinted.

Match Stamp—A match tax stamp used for collecting revenue.

Medicine Stamps—A medicine tax stamp used for collecting revenue.

Meter Cancellation—A machine used by the post office to apply and cancel postage at the same time, thereby speeding up the processing of mail and eliminating the use of the postage stamp.

Military Stamps—Stamps used by the armed forces of a nation at war which were issued solely for their purpose.

Millimeter (mm)—A metric unit of measurement used as an international standard to measure perforations. The perforation number is the number of perforations within 20mm.

Miniature Sheet—A souvenir sheet usually issued for a special occasion or exhibition; generally much smaller with large border; can also be one stamp or small block of stamps with special wording or design.

Minor Varieties—A tiny or trivial variation in design or color of a stamp.

Mint—An unused stamp; can also mean, in some cases, containing full original gum and never having been hinged.

Mount (Mounts)—Articles used to apply stamps to pages—*e.g.*, stamp hinges, acetate holders.

Natural Gum Skip—Streaking of original gum that appears disturbed, even though condition was caused "naturally" in the process of machine applying the original gum that was used. Often found in Zeppelin issues (C-13, C-14, C-15, C-18).

Net—Generally means "the total"; no deductions allowed; the full amount.

Never Hinge—Stamp in original "post office condition," having original gum that has never been disturbed by a hinge or other type of stamp mount.

New Issue—Latest issue; new stamps.

Newspaper Stamps—Stamps especially used to prepay postage on newspapers.

Nibs—The perforation teeth on a stamp; the tips of the perfs.

Numerical Cancellation—Early U.S. stamp cancellations in which a number was used.

Obliteration—Cancellation mark.

Obsolete—Series of stamps no longer being sold at the post office or by their agencies.

Off Center—Design of a stamp that is not equidistant from its borders or margins; not printed "on center" of stamp's face.

Officials—Governmental department stamps issued for officials' use.

Official Seal—A post office departmental label, issued in stamp form to seal mail and parcel post that has been damaged in shipment; may also be used by postal inspectors to re-seal packages opened for postal inspection.

Off Paper—Stamps removed from paper by soaking.

Offset Lithography—The modern lithography process which consists of transferring an image etched or photographically reproduced on a metal plate to a rubber blanket, then to a piece of paper from the rubber blanket.

On Cover—The original envelope with stamp bearing an original postmark.

On Piece—Pertaining to a stamp or stamps on a part of an envelope or folded cover.

Original—"Not a reprint" of an issue, but the first-issue stamp.

Original Gum (O.G.)—The original gum or adhesive applied at the mint at the time a stamp is printed by the post office department.

Over-Print—The additional printing applied to a first issue after the first issue was printed. Good examples are Kansas and Nebraska over-print issues.

Oxidized—The darkening of a stamp by exposure to the elements; caused sometimes by sulfurization with age.

Pair—Two stamps that have not been separated; joined vertically or horizontally—*e.g.*, vertical pair; horizontal pair.

Pane—Each press sheet of stamps is divided into 4 panes; the smaller stamps are printed 400 stamps per sheet, then cut into 100 stamps per pane; each large stamp sheet (commemoratives) comes with 200 stamps per sheet, and a pane would consist of 50 stamps.

Paper—Used to hold the design of a stamp; comes from several natural sources: cotton, silk, or wood pulp. May or may not have a watermark. Common varieties:

- Woven Paper—most popular of papers; a smooth, even finish without watermark; suitable for all types of printing
- India Paper—opaque thin stock
- Porous Paper—absorbent paper
- Chalky Paper—a chalk- or clay-coated paper

Parcel Post—Parcels sent through the post office.

Part Original Gum—Stamp showing part of the original gum, while the other portion of gum is either covered by a hinge remnant or gum is not present at all.

Part Perforated—Can refer to stamps with straight edges, but generally means any stamp that is not perforated on all 4 sides.

Pen Cancellation—Stamp's cancellation that has been applied with pen and ink.

Perf—Perforation abbreviation.

Perf Initials—For the purpose of preventing stealing in offices where postage stamps are used in large quantities. The stamps are impressed with perforated initials of the user; also called "punch-perforated stamps."

Perforation Gauge—Measuring instrument used to determine the number of perforation holes within a 20mm space.

Perforations—Tiny holes in a sheet of stamps that make separation of the stamps into individual stamps possible without the use of a cutting instrument or scissors.

Perforation Thin—Perforation has original gum and part of paper removed so that area appears thinner than rest of the stamp; often visible in watermark detector.

Permit—Commercial user's license number issued by post office for bulk mailing of postage. Paid in cash by user at the time mail is delivered for mailing to the post office. License number is preprinted in upper right-hand area of envelope.

Philatelic (fill-a-tell-ic)—Adjective for philately.

Philatelic Agency—Post office department agency

charged with the duty of supplying stamps to stamp collectors and dealers from specially selected stock of well-centered material.

Philatelic Foundation—Reputable organization used as a source to authenticate stamps as to their condition and to verify that issue is genuine. For more information, write to:

Philatelic Foundation
270 Madison Avenue,
New York, New York 10016

Philatelist—A "philatelic" student; a stamp collector.

Philately (fill-ate-ill-ee)—Name given the study of postage stamps by M. Herpin of Paris, France (1865).

Photogravure—Design of stamp photographed on the printing plate through fine screen breaking the copy up into fine dots that are square in shape. Ink is held by the depressions formed around the squares, thereby making it a very rapid, successful form of printing.

Pictorials—Stamps with illustrated scenes, as opposed to portraits of famous people.

Pigeon Post—Postage paid on mail carried by carrier pigeon (primarily used in New Zealand).

Plate—Flat metal piece etched, photoengraved, or hand-engraved with image for printing process. Plates are made with copper, zinc, or steel.

Plate Number—Number engraved on plate which appears on a sheet of stamps as its file number for purposes of maintaining accurate records in stamp-printing plants.

Plate Number Block—A block of stamps bearing a plate number that has been removed from a sheet with its sheet margin still attached.

Plate Proof—A plate impression printed as a sample prior to the actual printing run of the issue.

Postage—Post office charge for transporting a letter through the mail.

Postage and Revenue—Stamp that can be used for revenue tax purposes or postage (found on many stamps).

Postage Due—Letters or parcels arriving at their destination with insufficient postage are charged to the receiver, usually by affixing "postage-due stamps" to the article mailed.

Postal Cancellation—Stamp bearing a cancellation which shows that it has been used for postage and not revenue or tax purposes.

Postal-Fiscal Stamps—Revenue stamps used as postage stamps.

Postally Used—Stamps used for postage only.

Postal Markings—Handstamp or machine markings applied to mail matter.

Postal Savings Stamps—For use in the postal savings system of the government.

Postal Stationery—Postcards, airmail letter sheets, and envelopes impressed with postage sold by the post office.

Postmark—Post office marking applied to letter or parcel, giving city, state, and date article was received by post office.

Postmaster Provisionals—Early stamps issued by postmasters prior to general issues printed by the government.

Precancels—Cancellation of stamps with city and state prior to being used on mail. When precanceled at the Bureau of Printing and Engraving, they are called Bureau Prints. If done at local post offices, they are known as local precancels.

Prexies—Presidential Series of Stamps—1938 nickname.

Private Proprietary Stamps—Issued to pay the revenue on products of private firms; firms involved were permitted to print their own stamps in order to pay the tax on matches, medicine, etc.

Proof—For inspection purposes, a strike from a new printing plate is taken to ascertain that everything is satisfactory before going to a large press run on the finished work.

Proprietary Stamps—See Private Proprietary Stamps.

Provisional Issue—Pending completion of a regular issue, a temporary issue of stamps is placed in use.

Pulled Perforation—A perforation that is not present on the stamp; a missing perforation.

Punch-Perforated Stamps—See Perf Initials.

Quadrille—An album page or stamp book page for making different arrangements with stamps using faintly ruled square guidelines.

Railroad Cancel—A railway mail car cancellation applied to mail on the car.

Railway Mail Service (R.M.S.)—Post office department division handling the mails carried by the railroads.

Railway Post Office (R.P.O.)—Post office facilities found in a railway station for expediting mail carried by train.

Recess Printed—A printing process in which the inked image is below the surface of the printing plate, putting a raised image on the stamp.

Re-cut—The retouching or re-engraving of a printing plate.

Red Cross Stamps—Semi-postal stamps issued to benefit the Red Cross organization.

Registration Stamps—Issued for payment of registration fees *only*.

Regular Issue—Issues that are for regular use over long periods of time; not a commemorative or air mail stamp.

Re-Gumming—The application of gum on a stamp that was not of the "orig-issue."

Re-Issue—A reprinting of an obsolete issue.

Repaired—A stamp that has had a fault expertly corrected or added—*e.g.*, a tear repaired, a perf added, or a thin filled.

Re-perforated—A straight-edge stamp that has been expertly perforated to specification.

Reprints—Stamps printed from the original plates after they have become obsolete.

Revenue Stamps—Stamps issued to pay internal revenue taxes of various types; also called a "fiscal."

Rocket Mail—Experimental rockets attempting to carry the mail.

Rosbach—The brand name of a perforating machine tested by the Bureau of Printing and Engraving; first tested on 1¢ Washington head of 1919; stamp was offset-printed, then perfed 12½.

Rotary Press Printing—The curved-plate printing of stamps on a rotary press. These stamps are slightly wider or longer than stamps printed of the same design on a flat press from flat printing plates.

Rouletting—The separation of stamps in a sheet that is different from perforation. It can be done several different ways, including with a toothed wheel cutter found on the printing press which makes 1/8″ slits between which were 1/16″ spaces.

Safety Paper—A forgery-proof paper of various types; similar to paper used to mint U.S. dollar bills, having silk threads within it.

Seals—Labels in the form of stamps used to promote or advertise many events, like stamp exhibitions, World's Fairs, Olympic Games, etc.

Secret Marks—Found in U.S. issues of 1873. Small marks are used for identification which must be detected by the use of a magnifying glass.

Selvage—Outer border of a pane of stamps that is the excess paper bearing plate numbers and bureau information, and registration marks of printing plate.

Semi-Postal Issues—Fund-raising variety of issues often called "charity stamps"; used for charitable purposes, the semi-postal stamps are for postal purposes, but a small portion of the face value goes to charity.

Series—A set of stamps which covers a subject or idea through various denominations (*e.g.*, National Park Series, George Washington Bicentennial Issue of 1932, Panama Pacific Exposition Issue of 1913, etc.).

Sesquicentennial—Commemorative stamps that celebrate the 150th anniversary of a special occasion or event (*e.g.*, Scott #835—3¢ Constitution ratification of 1938 issue).

Set—A series of stamps which covers the smallest to the largest denomination of an issue with a complete account of those found between them having a similarity of design or concept which each issue relates to. (Several examples are the pictorial issues of 1869—Scott #112–122; Columbian Issues of 1893—Scott #230–245; Pan-American Exposition Issues of 1901—

Scott #294–299, etc. Each would be a set, excluding error or inverts.)

Se-Tenant—Two or more stamps joined together which were purposely printed to have: 1. different colors; 2. different denominations; 3. different surcharges; 4. different overprints; 5. different designs; etc.

Shade—Different intensities of a color of the same stamp caused by a number of conditions, like inconsistencies of quality control in ink from manufacturers; change in ink-feeder operators; press make-ready.

Sheet of Stamps—A full sheet of paper on which 2 or 4 "panes" of stamps have been printed; sheet is cut into its "panes" in order to ship to post office for official sale. "Panes" are often incorrectly called "sheets," by novice and professional alike.

Ship Cancellation—Mail canceled on board a ship which bears its postmark.

Short Perforation—Perforation that is smaller than the rest on the stamp, caused by careless separation of stamps on sheet, pane, or block.

Souvenir Sheet—Special sheets of stamps issued for stamp exhibitions or other special events; often in "miniature" sheet form a few stamps will appear within a large paper margin (*e.g.*, Scott #735—Issues of 1934 National Stamp Exhibition Issue Souvenir Sheet).

Space Filler—Usually a faulty stamp which is used as a substitute for a "sound" copy of the same issue in order to "fill the space" vacant in a collector's album until a better copy is acquired to replace it.

Special-Delivery Stamps—Issues used to pay for the extra service in delivering mail that is not held until the regularly scheduled time of delivery.

Special-Handling Stamps—Issues used on parcel post, giving the package first-class handling.

Specialist—A collector or investor who specializes in a particular area of interest for personal pleasure or heavy investment gain (*e.g.*, collector specialists—boats, countries, flowers, horses, sports, etc.).

Investor specialists—Scott #

all	all	all
1	2	245

All inverts, all U.S. Zepps.

Specialize—Area covered by the specialist (*e.g.*, collector specialists—horses, flowers, sports, country collections, etc.; investor specialists—Scott #1, #2, #292, #293, #241–245, # inverts).

Specimen Stamps—"Specimen"-marked stamps are distributed to Universal Postal Union members. They are taken from the initial printing run.

Speck—Blemish or dot appearing on surface or back as indicated.

Stain—A discoloration that is not the normal coloring of a stamp.

Stampless Covers—Envelopes without stamps that were mailed before stamps were invented, having postmarks and other markings applied by the postmaster.

Straight Edge—A stamp having 1 or 2 straight edges coming from the side or corner of a sheet or pane. Other issues of the sheet would be perforated on all 4 sides (not a coil).

Strip—Three or more stamps vertically or horizontally joined by their perforations.

Surcharge—Found on foreign stamps (not found on U.S. ones) where the name of a country or the value has been changed on an existing stamp.

Surtax—Often an "overprint" on a regular issue in which additional face value has been added on a semi-postal stamp over and above the amount that covers postage for its normal purpose.

Telegraph Stamps—Stamps used in payment of telegram or telegraph fees that were issued by telegraph companies (*e.g.*, Western Union Telegraph Co.).

Tercentenary—300th anniversary celebration.

Tête-bêche Stamps—Unsevered pair of stamps—having one right side up, the other upside down.

Thinned—Defect in a stamp where the thickness of the paper has been diminished as a result of improper hinge removal. A light area appears when the stamp is held up to a bright light, or a dark area appears when the stamp is placed in a watermark detector.

Tied to Cover—A stamp or group of stamps on an envelope that bears a postmark which is on the stamp and envelope, showing that the stamps were originally used to mail that particular envelope. Stamps on an envelope with this type of "tieing" are often worth more than they would be off the piece.

Tongs—A simple hand tweezers used as a tool to handle stamps without touching them by hand (*e.g.*, round end, flat square, simple tip).

Topicals—Stamps with particularly related subject matter in a special area of collecting (*e.g.*, fish stamps, flag stamps, horse stamps, flower stamps, etc.).

Trial Color—A test (essay) to determine final approval of color prior to issue being run.

Trivial—Not important, insignificant (usually mentioned for accuracy).

Typeset Stamps—Stamps produced using ordinary printer's type.

Typographed—Printing from movable type or from engraved plates on which the design printed is raised above the level.

Unaddressed—Having no address.

United Nation Stamps—Stamps issued by nations of the world striving for peace and world understanding; sold only within the building of the United Nations in New York City, but used anywhere in the world for postage purposes.

Universal Postal Union (U.P.U.)—It is made up of all the civilized nations of the world and is the means for exchanging all international mail. It was organized by Dr. Von Stephan in 1974 in Berne, Switzerland.

Unused—A stamp that is mint and never used for postage; therefore, it is uncanceled.

Unwatermarked—Paper bearing no watermark upon which the stamps are printed.

Used—A canceled stamp that was used to pay the postage on a letter or parcel.

Value—Pertaining to "cash market value," "catalogue value," or "face value."

Variety—Having multiple differences within the same issue; generally pertaining to coloration.

Vertical—Being perpendicular to the horizon; upright in design; used to describe coil stamps that have perforations on the horizontal sides and straight edges on the "vertical" sides.

Vertical Crease—A crease in the stamp running vertically across the design of the stamp.

Vertical Pair—Two stamps vertically joined.

Very Light Hinge—Almost-invisible mark left on original gum of stamp after removal of hinge in which gum remains totally intact, but still not enough to merit "never hinge" status.

War Tax Stamps—Issues used on mail during war periods having additional tariff which pays a war tax to help the nation's war effort.

Watermark—An impression found in the paper of a printed stamp, having a pattern, letter, word, or other mark—used for identification purposes.

Watermark Detector—A device used to detect a watermark in a stamp. It is a black shallow tray containing a solution of benzine, carbon tetrachloride, or carbona. The stamp is dropped face down and soaked in it. The watermark will appear if it bears one.

Wells Fargo—Company that operated the early stage coach routes which carried the mail, freight, gold, and passengers to and from the West (around the mid-1800s).

Wine Stamps—Treasury Department stamps issued to pay internal revenue tax on wines.

Zepps—Referring to Zeppelin-bearing stamps.

Zeppelin Stamps—To commemorate the flight of the Graff Zeppelin and other similar airships. Stamps were used in connection with postage carried by the Zeppelin. Covers carried were known as "Zeppelin covers."

APPENDIX IV

SYMBOLS AND ABBREVIATIONS

✳		Mint
⊙		Used
▲		on piece
⊞		Block
⊠		cover
//		incomplete
addr.		address
appear.		appearance
B		Bottom
bklt		booklet
blk		block
BPA		British Philatelic Association
b/s		backstamp
canc.		cancel (cancellation)
cat.		catalogue
c/c		corner card
cds		circular date stamp
cent'd		centered
cent'g		centering
certif.		certificate
commem		commemorative
cond		condition
cplt		complete
cr		crease or creased
cvr		cover
D		Document
dbl		double
DCDS		double circular date stamp

defin		definitive
dist.		disturbed
distrb.		disturbed
DL wmk		double-line watermark
ds		date stamp
dup.		duplicate
E.		Essay
ECV		Estimated Cash Value
Env		Envelope
Est.		Estimate
FDC		First-Day Cover
FF		First Flight
FFC		First-Flight Cover
FL		folded letter
H		hinged
H canc.		heavy cancel
HH		heavy hinge
HHR		heavy hinge remnant
horz.		horizontal
horz. cr.		horizontal crease
HR		hinge remnant
h/s		handstamp
imperf		imperforate
impt		imprint
incl		included

SYMBOLS AND ABBREVIATIONS

inscrip —————— inscrip-
    tion
inv —————— inverted

L —————— Left
lg —————— large
LH —————— light hinge
Line pr —————— Line pair
LL —————— lower left
LR —————— lower right
lt —————— light

mgn —————— margin
min. —————— minimum
ms. —————— manuscript
ms. canc. —————— pen can-
    cellation done by hand
mtd —————— mounted

NG —————— no gum
NGS —————— Natural
    Gum Skip
NH —————— never hinged
nibbed —————— short per-
    foration
norm —————— normal

o/ —— means "on" or "over"
octag —————— octagonal
OG —————— original gum
orig. —————— original
ovpt. —————— overprint
o/w —————— otherwise

P —————— proof
part OG —————— part
    original gum
perf —————— perforation
perf th —————— perfora-
    tion thin
PF —————— Philatelic
    Foundation
pl —————— plate
Pl Bk —————— plate block
pl # —————— plate num-
    ber

PM —————— postmaster
pmk. —————— postmark
pos —————— position
poss. —————— possible
poss. re-gum —————— pos-
    sible regumming
pp —————— pulled perfor-
    ation
PPC —————— picture
    postcard
pr —————— pair
p/s —————— postal
    stationery
ptg —————— printing

R —————— right
recv'd —————— received
reg'd —————— registered
reg'y —————— registry
regum —————— regum-
    ming
rev —————— revenue
roul —————— roulette
RPS —— Royal Philatelic Society
    (London)

S —————— specimen
sc —————— scrape
se —————— straight edge
selv. —————— selvage
sgl. —————— single
sht —————— sheet
S/L —————— straight line
SL wmk —————— straight-
    line watermark
sm —————— small
sp —————— short perfor-
    ation
spk —————— speck
SS —————— Souvenir
    Sheet
stn —————— stain
stp —————— strip
surch —————— surcharge

T —————— top

TC	trial color	vert. cr	vertical crease
th	thinned	vert. pr	vertical pair
triv.	trivial	VLH	very light hinge
U	upper		
UL	upper left		
unaddr	unaddressed	w/	with
unwmk'd	unwatermarked	wmk	watermarked
UR	upper right	w/o	without
val.	value		
var	variety	Zepps	Zeppelin (stamps bearing images of inflated airships)
vert.	vertical		

APPENDIX V

PHILATELIC ASSOCIATIONS

PUBLISHERS OF UNITED STATES AND WORLDWIDE STAMP CATALOGUES

American Air Mail
  Society
Gerhard Wolff
C/O Elmer Fox
Westheimer & Co.
540 Investment Bldg.
Washington, DC 20005

American Philatelic
  Society
P. O. Box 800
State College, PA 16801

American Revenue
  Association
Sherwood Springer
3761 West 117th St.
Hawthorne, CA 90250

American Stamp Dealers'
  Association
840 Willis Avenue
Albertson, NY 11507

Arabian Philatelic
  Association
Aramco Box 1929
Dhahran, Saudi Arabia

Brazil Philatelic
  Association
T. E. Gaughan
Thompson Drive
Washingtonville, NY
  10992

Bureau Issues Association
16 Sammis Lane
White Plains, NY 10605

Canadian Stamp Dealers'
  Association
L. A. Davenport
7 Jackes Avenue,
  Apt. 308
Toronto, Ontario
  M4T 1E3 Canada

Canal Zone Study Group
Alfred R. Bew, Secretary
20 South South Carolina
  Avenue
Atlantic City, NJ 08401

China Stamp Society
Ellery Denison, President
7207 Thirteenth Place
Takoma Park, MD 20012

Confederate Stamp
  Alliance
Jack Solomon
612 East Park Avenue
Long Beach, NY 11561

Costa Rica Collectors,
  Society of
Route 3, Box 72
Marbel Falls, TX 78654

Croatian Philatelic
  Society
260 Vancouver Street
London, Ontario
N5W 4R8 Canada

Czechoslovak Philately,
  Society for
87 Carmita Avenue
Rutherford, NJ 07070

Eire Philatelic
  Association
John J. Blessington,
  Secretary
4302 St. Clair Avenue
Studio City, CA 91604

Estonian Philatelic
  Society
Rudolf Hamar, President
243 East 34th Street
New York, NY 10016

France & Colonies
  Philatelic Society
Walter Parshall,
  Secretary
103 Spruce Street
Bloomfield, NJ 07003

Friedl Expert Committee
10 East 40th Street
New York, NY 10016

Germany Philatelic
  Society
c/o Fred Behrendt,
  Secretary
P. O. Box 563
Westminster, MD 21157

Guatemala Collectors,
  International Society of
Richard Canman,
  President
175 West Jackson
  Boulevard
Chicago, IL 60604

Hellenic Philatelic,
  Society of America
Maurice R. Friend, M.D.,
  Secretary
262 Central Park West
New York, NY 10024

Japanese Philately,
International Society of
Lois M. Evans, Secretary
P. O. Box 961
State College, PA 16801

Korea Stamp Society
Forrest W. Calkins,
  Secretary
P. O. Box 1057
Grand Junction,
  CO 81501

Mexico-Elmhurst
Philatelic Society
International
Mrs. Judith Saks
2310 Veteran
West Los Angeles,
CA 90064

Netherlands Philatelic
Society
Julius Mansbach,
Secretary
6323 North Francisco
Chicago, IL 60645

Oceania Philatelic
Society
William Hagan, President
1523 East Meadowbrook
Drive
Loveland, OH 45140

Philatelic Foundation
270 Madison Avenue
New York, NY 10016

Polonus Philatelic Society
864 North Ashland
Avenue
Chicago, IL 60622

Portuguese Philately,
International
Society for
Robert L. Huggins
69 Woodland Avenue,
Glen Ridge, NJ 07028

Rossica, Society of
Russian Philately
Norman Epstein,
Treasurer
33 Crooke Avenue
Brooklyn, NY 11226

El Salvador, Associated
Collectors of
Joseph D. Hahn
P. O. Box 522
State College, PA 16801

Scandinavian Collectors'
Club
Box 175
Ben Franklin Station
Washington, DC 20044

Scott Publishing
Company
530 Fifth Avenue
New York, NY 10036

Society of Philatelic
Americans
Robert B. Brandeberry
P. O. Box 9041
Wilmington, DE 19809

United Postal Stationery
Society
Central Office
P. O. Box 1407
Bloomington, IL 61701

APPENDIX VI

RETAIL STAMP STORES

Note: Listed here is a selection of retailers trading through stores. All are members in good standing of the American Stamp Dealers' Association, Inc., 840 Willis Avenue, Albertson, NY 11507.

ALABAMA

M & M Stamp Company
7914 Memorial Parkway,
   SW Suite 15
Huntsville, AL 35802

ALASKA

North Pole Stamps
802 "D" Street
Anchorage, AK 99501

ARIZONA

ABA Philatelic Center
P. O. Box 4190
Scottsdale, AZ 85258

American Philatelic
   Brokerages, Inc.
7225 N. Oracle Rd.
Tucson, AZ 85704

Arizona Stamp &
   Coin Co.
4668 E. Speedway
Tucson, AZ 85712

Robert S. Freeman
7809 North 37th Avenue
Phoenix, AZ 85021

Leon B. Parker
3180 E. Indian
   School Rd.
Phoenix, AZ 85016

Old Pueblo Stamp Shop
6666 East Broadway
Tucson, AZ 85710

Utopia Stamp Co.
7217 East Main St.
Scottsdale, AZ 85251

ARKANSAS

Joseph E. Bateman Jr.
11500 Rodney Parham,
   Suite 21
Little Rock, AR 72212

CALIFORNIA

Aljim Stamps
10919 No. Wolfe Rd.
Cupertino, CA 95014

Frank L. Allard Jr.
P. O. Bin 4526
Carmel-by-the-Sea,
    CA 93921

N. F. Ausdenmoore
7953 Auburn Blvd.
Citrus Heights, CA 95610

Blackburn & Blackburn
    Ltd.
Junipero and 6th
P. O. Box 7246
Carmel-by-the-Sea,
    CA 93921

Brewart Stamps
403 West Katella
Anaheim, CA 92802

Classic Philatelics
2207 Main Street, #31
Huntington Beach,
    CA 92648

Cliffco Consolidated
    Corp.
155 East Third St.
Chico, CA 95926

Coast Philatelics
1113-D Baker St.
Costa Mesa, CA 92626

Coin & Stamp World
    Ltd.
17519 Chatsworth St.
Granada Hills, CA 91344

Fred Coops Stamp &
    Coin Galleries
115 Central City Mall
San Bernardino,
    CA 92401

James H. Crum
2720 East Gage Ave.
Huntington Park,
    CA 90255

Burton Doling
P. O. Box 5044
Sherman Oaks, CA 91413

Robert Elliot
1624 Seabright Avenue
Santa Cruz, CA 95062

Fireside Stamp Co.
3530 Grand Ave.
Oakland, CA 94610

Joe Forrester
2100 16th St.
Sacramento, CA 95818

Lester S. Glass
1553 So. La Cienaga
    Blvd.
Los Angeles, CA 90035

Globe Stamp Store
2126 Center St.
Berkeley, CA 94704

Sidney S. Golditch
969 Grand Ave.
San Rafael, CA 94901

O. J. Izdepski
8015 Sunset Ave.
Fair Oaks, CA 95628

Kenrich Co.
9416 Las Tunas Drive
Temple City, CA 91780

Mid-Valley Stamp Shop
3321 McHenry, Suite G
Modesto, CA 95350

Miracle Mile Stamp
Center
5613 Wilshire Blvd.
Los Angeles, CA 90036

Natick Store
209 W. 4th St.
Los Angeles, CA 90013

Pacific Stamp & Coin
Sales
8839 La Suvida Drive
La Mesa, CA 92041

Pasadena Stamp
Company
1000 East Walnut St.
Pasadena, CA 91106

Stanley M. Piller
3351 Grand Ave.
Oakland, CA 94601

Shnayer's Philatelic
Services, Inc.
1420 Mangrove Ave.
Chico, CA 95296

Don W. Soper
73-885 Highway 111,
Suite 5
Palm Desert, CA 92260

The Stamp Shoppe
1156 Laurel St.
San Carlos, CA 94070

The Stamp Tree, Inc.
701 High St., 216
Auburn, CA 95603

Superior Stamp & Coin
Co., Inc.
9301 Wilshire Blvd.
Beverly Hills, CA 90210

William C. Tatham
Stamp Co.
6727 S. Washington Ave.
Whittier, CA 90608

United States Stamp Co.
368 Bush St.
San Francisco, CA 94104

Wester Philatelix, Inc.
3868 Carson St., #107
Torrance, CA 90503

Richard Wolffers, Inc.
127 Kearny St.
San Francisco, CA 94108

COLORADO

Richard D. Clark
1545 Glenarm Pl., #406
Denver, CO 80202

Bill Hurd Stamps
9078 East LeHigh
Denver, CO 80237

L & L Coin & Stamp
5500 W. 44th Ave.
Denver, CO 80212

Monument Stamps
805 N. First St.
(Box 2166)
Grand Junction,
CO 81501

James B. Peterson
9818 East Colfax Ave.
Aurora, CO 80010

Rocky Mountain Stamp
Supplies
1545 Glenarm Pl.
Denver, CO 80202

Christopher Swinbank
1545 Glenarm Pl.,
  Suite 214
Denver, CO 80202

CONNECTICUT

City Stamp Expo
1185 So. Main St.
Cheshire, CT 06410

Miller's Stamp Shop
41 New London
  Turnpike
Uncasville, CT 06382

Parcel Poste Company
25 Newtown Rd.
(Route 6)
Danbury, CT 08610

DISTRICT OF COLUMBIA

Uptown Stamps (Capital
  Philatelics)
3416 Connecticut Ave.
  NW
Washington, DC 20008

FLORIDA

Arlington Stamp &
  Coin Co.
1350 University Blvd. N.
Jacksonville, FL 32211

Richard Basini
3045 North Federal
  Highway, 60-C
Fort Lauderdale,
  FL 33306

The Browse House
P. O. Box 421
Holly Hill, FL 32017

Court Street Stamp &
  Coin
125 Court St.
Clearwater, FL 33516

Ricardo Delcampo
206 S. E. First Ave.
Miami, FL 33131

Gulfcoast Coin Brokers,
  Inc.
1678 Colonial Blvd.
Fort Myers, FL 33907

John W. McDaniel Jr.,
  Inc.
210 Park Ave. N., Suite 1
Winter Park, FL 32789

Robert J. Murrin, Inc.
7500 49th St. N.
Pinellas Park, FL 33565

New England Stamp
643 Fifth Ave. S.
Naples, FL 33940

Michael Rogers, Inc.
340 Park Ave. N.
Winter Park, FL 33568

William G. Rose
33 Fourth St. N.
St. Petersburg, FL 33701

Sears Stamp & Coin
  Dept.
Sears Countryside Mall
2601 U.S. 19 North
Clearwater, FL 33515

Tippett, Inc.
1469 Main St.
Sarasota, FL 33577

GEORGIA

Bargain Bob
c/o Journeys End
"On the Square"
Dahlonega, GA 30533

George Stamp & Coin
Co.
129 Carnegie Way, N.W.
Atlanta, GA 30303

Robert Loewenthal,
United States Stamps
2095 Mountain Creek
Court
Stone Mountain,GA 30087
Stamps Unlimited of
Georgia, Inc.
133 Carnegie Way N.W.,
Room 203
Atlanta, GA 30303

IDAHO

Mary B. Pyle (The Stamp
House)
2415 Madison
Boise, ID 83702

Wilson A & B—U.S.
Stamps
2127 Toluka Way
Boise, ID 83702

ILLINOIS

Perry E. Arnquist
604 Hollister Ave.
Rockford, IL 61108

B-K Stamp Shoppe
652 West Stephenson St.
Freeport, IL 61032

Bob's Stamps & Coins
4407 Milwaukee Ave.
Chico, IL 60630

Bollmeier Hobby Shop
715 East Main
Belleville, IL 62221

Carson Pirie Scott & Co.
1 South State St.
Chicago, IL 60603

Chandler's Inc.
630 Davis St.
Evanston, IL 60204

Cherryvale Coins &
Stamps
F139 Cherryvale Mall
Rockford, IL 61112

Great Lakes Stamp
Auctions
6687 Northwest Highway
Chicago, IL 60631

Liberty Stamp Shop, Inc.
314-16 S. Dearborn St.
Chicago, IL 60604

Mitch's Stamps & Coins/
6333 W. Cermak Rd.
Berwyn, IL 60402

Peoria Stamp Center
613 W. Glen
Peoria, IL 61614

Edward V. Provost
4859 S. Luna Ave.
Chicago, IL 60638

Rasdale Stamp Co.
36 S. State St.
Chicago, IL 60603

John G. Ross
12 West Madison St.
Chicago, IL 60602

Sandler Bros.
3938 No. Pulaski
Chicago, IL 60641

Stamp King
600 Higgins Rod.
Park Ridge, IL 60068

Stereo Stamps
3109 No. Milwaukee Ave.
Chicago, IL 60618

Strauss Coins & Stamps,
Inc.
P. O. Box 95337
Schaumberg, IL 60195

Thomas M. Tomc,
Specialist
714 N. Wells St.
Chicago, IL 60610

INDIANA

The Town Crier
P. O. Box 271
Nashville, IN 47448

KANSAS

Suburban Stamp Gallery
5010 Linden
Mission, KS 66205

LOUISIANA

B. B. & B. Stamps
P. O. Box 8791
Shreveport, LA 71108

Charles "Sandy" Ewing
3908 MacArthur Drive
P. O. Box 57773
Alexandria, LA 71310

The Little Stamp
Company
5101 W. Esplanade Ave.
Metairie, LA 70002

MAINE

Charles Seaman
34 Pine Hill Rd.
Box 817
Ogunquist, ME 03907

MARYLAND

Roy Cox
Box 3610
Baltimore, MD 21214

Arch Handy
310 N. Main St.
Bel Air, MD 21014

Ken Stamps & Antiques, Inc.
26 Winter St.
Hagerstown, MD 21740

Maryland Stamps & Coins
7720 Wisconsin Ave.
Bethesda, MD 20014

MASSACHUSETTS

Battle Green Stamp & Coin
4 Muzzey St.
Lexington, MA 02173

J. M. Blood, Inc.
380 High St.
Holyoke, MA 01040

Collector Shop, Inc.
865 Boylston St.
Boston, MA 02116

Fall River Stamp & Coin Co.
17 Second St.
Fall River, MA 02720

H. E. Haris & Co., Inc.
645 Summer St.
Boston, MA 02210

Norman C. Hinds Jr., Inc.
19 Inn St.
Newburyport, MA 01950

Max C. Kaye
311 Bridge St.
Springfield, MA 01103

LnL Stamps
105 N. Main St.
Randolph, MA 02368

Norumbega Stamp Company
84 Pleasant St.
South Natick, MA 01760

Patriot Stamps
P.O. Box 233
Lincoln, MA 01773

Suburban Stamps, Inc.
P. O. Box 715
115 Progress Ave.
Springfield, MA 01101

Westminster Stamp Gallery, Inc.
P. O. Box 447
Norfolk, MA 02056

MICHIGAN

Birmingham Stamps & Coins, Inc.
1287 S. Woodward
Birmingham, MI 48011

Jack Frimodig, "Stamps for Collectors"
106 S. Washington
Saginaw, MI 48607

Frank J. Kengel
89 S. Gratiot
Mt. Clemens, MI 48043

Robert E. Lippert Co.
23800 Gretaer Mack
St. Clair Shores, MI 48080

MINNESOTA

Hamernick Stamp Co.
522 Rice St.
St. Paul, MN 55103

Maltalately (Andy's
Stamps)
125 N. Seventh St.
Minneapolis, MN 55403

Minnesota Stamp Co.
129½ E. First Ave.
(Box 218)
Shakopee, MN 55379

Plaza Stamps & Coins,
Inc.
3939 West 50th St.
Edina, MN 55424

MISSOURI

Knight's Coins Stamps &
Supplies
323 South Avenue
Springfield, MO 65806

K-T Stamps, Inc.
Box 8472
Kansas City, MO 64114

St. Louis Stamp & Coin
Co.
Suite 351
818 Olive St.
St. Louis, MO 63101

The Stamp Corner
8145 Delmar Blvd.
St. Louis, MO 63130

MONTANA

Montana Coin & Stamp
2818 Third Ave. N.
Billings, MT 59101

NEBRASKA

Aksarben Stamps
10817 Prairie Brook Rd.
Omaha, NB 68144

NEVADA

Shelly Bialac
3661 Maryland Parkway
Las Vegas, NV 89109

Robert L. Faiman
3645 Las Vegas Blvd. S.
Las Vegas, NV 89109

T. and A. Stamp & Coin
Ltd.
118 W. Second St.
Suite 14A
Reno, NV 89501

NEW HAMPSHIRE

Richard D. Dolloff
116 State St.
Portsmouth, NH 03801

NEW MEXICO

Stamp Collectors Center,
Inc.
3601 San Mateo N. E.
Albuquerque, NM 87110

NEW JERSEY

Samuel August
1776 Springfield Ave.
Maplewood, NJ 07040

B & C Stamp Co.
7 West Main St.
Somerville, NJ 08876

Downtown Stamp Co.
44 Academy St.
Newark, NJ 07102

Fairidge Stamp Co.
11 North Broad St.
Ridgewood, NJ 07450

William A. Fox
263 White Oak Ridge Rd.
Short Hills, NJ 07078

James Keltie
1021 Michigan Ave.
Cape May, NJ 08204

Joseph Lowinger
1073 Stuyvesant Ave.
Irvington, NJ 07111

M. Meghrig & Sons
145 Coolidge Ave.
Englewood, NJ 07631

Monmouth Stamp &
Coin Shop
39 Monmouth St.
Red Bank, NJ 07701

Tadson Stamps & Coins
31 Village Square
Bergen Mall
Paramus, NJ 07652

The Washington Press
1776 Springfield Ave.
Maplewood, NJ 07040

NEW YORK

Allied Stamp Co.
160 W. 46th St.
New York, NY 10036

Almar Stamps
242-09 Northern Blvd.
Douglaston, NY 11363

Arrow Stamp & Coin
Center
82 Rockaway Ave.
Valley Stream, NY 11580

Barrett's Exchange
P. O. Box 188
Ithaca, NY 14850

Emmanuel G. Brooks
2601 Avenue U
Brooklyn, NY 11229

Frank J. Buono
24 Fayette St.
Binghamton, NY 13901

David H. Burr
55 Prospect Ave.
Gloversville, NY 12078

Cherrystone Stamp
Center, Inc.
132 W. 34th St.
New York, NY 10001

Clearing House for
Stamps, Inc.
764 W. 181st St.
New York, NY 10033

Collectors Galleries, Inc.
256 Main St.
Huntington, NY 11743

Dumont Stamp Co., Inc.
907 Seventh Ave.
New York, NY 10019

Ed's Coins & Stamps
Sun-Vet Mall Shopping
  Center
8501 Sunrise Highway
Holbrook, NY 11741

Giant Stamp Store
122 Brighton 11 St.
Brooklyn, NY 11235

Grossman Stamp Co.,
860 Broadway
New York, NY 10003

Harbor Coins & Stamps
134 Mamaroneck Ave.
Mamaroneck, NY 10543

Huntington Stamp &
  Coin, Inc.
1060 E. Jericho Turnpike
Huntington, NY 11743

Jamestown Stamp Co.
341-3 East Third St.
Jamestown, NY 14701

Legion Stamps, Inc.
3774 Merrick Rd.
Seaford, NY 11783

Lindner Publications,
  Inc.
P. O. Box 922
Syracuse, NY 13201

McLeod Stamp Co., Inc.
2198 Monroe Ave.
Rochester, NY 14618

Marlen Stamps & Coins,
  Inc.
214-24 73rd Ave.
Bayside, NY 11364

Miller's Mint
313 East Main St.
Patchogue, NY 11772

Morowitz Stamps
147 W. 42nd St.
New York, NY 10036

Mosden Stamp Co., Inc.
232 E. 54th St.
New York, NY 10022

North Shore Stamp &
  Coin Exchange, Inc.
53A Cutter Mill Rd.
Great Neck, NY 11021

Daniel J. Nutzul
  (Penfield Stamp Shop)
1832 Penfield Rd.
Penfield, NY 14526

Omega Stamp & Coin
  Co.
1586 Flatbush Ave.
Brooklyn, NY 11210

Rego Stamp Co.
55 W. 42nd St.
New York, NY 10036

Joseph L. Rubin
Jody Stamp Studio, Inc.
6001A Riverdale Ave.
Riverdale, NY 10471

Brian Skinner, Inc.
245 E. 54th St.
New York, NY 10022

Syracuse Stamp & Coin
   Co.
122 E. Washington St.
Syracuse, NY 13202

Village Stamps
Box B
Whitesboro, NY 13492

NORTH CAROLINA

Cape Hatteras Stamp &
   Coin Co., Inc.
P. O. Box 9337
Greensboro, NC 27408

Raleigh Stamp Shop
P. O. Box 10092
Raleigh, NC 27605

OHIO

Freeman's Stamps
7581 Brandt Pike
Dayton, OH 45424

J. & D. Stamps, Inc.
P. O. Box 39291
Cincinnati, OH 45239

L. Kozorog Co.
Room 1303-04
1010 Euclid Ave.
Cleveland, OH 44115

Major Stamps
306 E. Beck St.
P. O. Box 808
Columbus, OH 43216

Marshall's Stamps &
   Coins
4608 Talmadge Rd.
Toledo, OH 43623

Greg and Randy Scholl
P. O. Box 123
Batavia, OH 45103

Thomas J. Woolley
2700 E. Dublin-Granville
   Rd., Suite 240
Columbus, OH 43229

OREGON

Cynthia E. Chase
P. O. Box 201
Salem, OR 97308

William K. Yoresen
4620 S. W. Washington
Beaverton, OR 97005

PENNSYLVANIA

Earl P. L. Apfelbaum,
   Inc.
2006 Walnut St.
Philadelphia, PA 19103

Harold W. Burton
P. O. Drawer E
Eagleville, PA 19408

Edelman's
301 York Road
Jenkintown, PA 19046

Richard Friedberg,
   Stamps
Masonic Bldg, Suite 337
Meadville, PA 16335

Hahn & Limoges, Inc.
119 South Fraser St.,
   Suite D
State College, PA 16801

Hobby & Craft Shop
Granite Run Mall
Media, PA 19063

Mill Dutkin, Inc.
111 South 18th St.
Philadelphia, PA 19103

Neshaminy Coins &
    Stamps
110 Neshaminy Mall
Cornwells Heights,
    PA 19020

Northeast Stamp & Coin
    Exchange Ltd.
Store 103B
LeHigh Valley Mall
Whitehall, PA 18052

Siegfried Pohl
916 W. Broad St.
Quakertown, PA 18951

Steinmetz Coins &
    Currency, Inc.
843 Park City
Lancaster, PA 17601

PUERTO RICO

Antilles Stamps
706 Miramar Ave.
Santurce, PR 00907

Caribe St. Center, Inc.
P. O. Box 2
Hato Rey, PR 00919

RHODE ISLAND

G. A. Feiner &
    Associates, Inc.
413 Kingstown Rd.
Wakefield, RI 02879

SOUTH CAROLINA

Rare Coin & Stamp
    Galleries
16 Gallery Center
Wade Hamilton Blvd.
Taylors, SC 29687

TEXAS

Adam's World of Hobbies
295 Westwood Mall
Houston, TX 77036

Bellaire Stamp & Coin
6819 Chimney Rock
Bellaire, TX 77401

Byron S. Brandt
5164 Broadway
San Antonio, TX 78209

The Coin Nook
Cullen Mall A-14
4803 S. Alameda
Corpus Christi, TX 78412

D. K. Stamp Co.
2201 North Tenth
Petite Mall
McAllen, TX 78501

Deaton's
206 West Thirteenth
Austin, TX 78701

Jack L. Frammell,
    Stamps & Coins
8304 Kate St.
Dallas, TX 75225

Sam Houston Philatelics,
    Inc.
14654 Memorial Drive
Houston, TX 77079

Magic Circle Coins &
  Stamps
5757 Westheimer #11
Houston, TX 77057

Metroplex Stamp Co.
1406B Main St.
Dallas, TX 75202

Rice Coin & Stamp Co.
4020 Westheimer
Houston, TX 77027

W. E. Shelton
5164 Broadway
San Antonio, TX 78209

Harry Stansbury, Stamps
Suite 258
Sharpstown Mall
7500 Bellaire Blvd.
Houston, TX 77036

Sun City Coin & Stamp
  Co., Inc.
87D Bassett Center
El Paso, TX 79925

Willis Stamp Center
4001 North Shepherd
Houston, TX 77018

TENNESSEE

John S. Turner
1748 Highland Ave. N.W.
Cleveland, TN 37311

VIRGINIA

The GalaStamp
  Organization
4914 Fitzhugh Ave.
Richmond, VA 23230

Old Dominio Stamp
  Sales, Inc.
380 Maple Ave. W.
Vienna, VA 22180

Packard Stamp Co.
13335 Midlothian
  Turnpike
Midlothian, VA 23113

Portside Stamps Ltd.
P. O. Box 145
Alexandria, VA 22313

Thalhimer's Stamps &
  Coins
650 East Broad St.
Richmond, VA 23219

WASHINGTON

Hepp's Stamp Shop
Room 203, Jones Bldg.
1331 Third Ave.
Seattle, WA 98101

Thomas Mechem
(Northwest Stamp Co.)
1750 Palm Ave. S. W.
Seattle, WA 98116

Melvin-Erickson, Inc.
(Hall's Stamp Shop)
P. O. Box 8095
Spokane, WA 99203

Noubar Nalbandian (The
  Stamp Hinge)
4728 University Way
  N.E.
Seattle, WA 98105

Rainier Philatelic, Inc.
15405 First Ave. S.
Seattle, WA 98148

John A. Schenk
1975 Marshall Ave.
Richland, WA 99352

Tacoma Stamp & Coin
  Shop
938 Commerce St.
Tacoma, WA 98402

S. W. Willard & Co.
1425 Fourth Ave.
Seattle, WA 98101

WISCONSIN

Northwestern Stamp Co.,
  Inc.
152 W. Wisconsin Ave.
Milwaukee, WI 53203

Steve Wood's Stamp
  Shop
4235 S. Howell Ave.
Milwaukee, WI 53207

APPENDIX VII

PHILATELIC PERIODICALS

Canadian Stamp News
1567 Sedlescomb Drive
Mississauga, Ontario L4X
  1M5, Canada

H. L. Lindquist
  Publications, Inc.
153 Waverly Place
New York, NY 10014

Linn's Stamp News
P. O. Box 29
Sidney, OH 45367

*Mekeel's Weekly Stamp
  News*
Box 1660
Portland, ME 04104

Minkus Stamp Journal
116 W. 32nd St.
New York, NY 10001

Western Stamp Collector
Box 10
Albany, OR 97321

APPENDIX VIII

AUCTION HOUSES

Advanced Philatelics
5410 Wilshire Blvd.
Los Angeles, CA 90036

George Alevizos Rare
   Stamps
320 Wilshire Blvd.
Santa Monica, CA 90401

Beck Stamp Auctions
P. O. Box 2216
Mesa, AZ 85204

Central Suffolk Auctions,
   Inc.
P. O. Box 33
Farmingville, NY 11738

Chandler's, Inc.
630 Davis St.
Evanston, IL 60204

Collector's Corner
P. O. Box 782
Detroit, MI 48232

Colonial Stamp Co.
5410 Wilshire Blvd.,
   Suite 202
Los Angeles, CA 90036

Ted Conway
P. O. Box 420
Lynboook, NY 11563

Downeast Stamps
52 Fern St.
Bangor, ME 04401

Dutch Country Auctions
c/o Robert L. Myers
P. O. Box 154
Coopersburg, PA 18036

E & F Stamp Auctions
Box 737
Marshalltown, IA 50158

F. E. Eaton & Sons Ltd.
6174 East Blvd.
Vancouver, BC V6M 3V6
Canada

Federal Stamp Co.
P. O. Box 7538
Fort Lauderdale,
   FL 33338

William A. Fox
263 White Oak Ridge Rd.
Short Hills, NJ 07078

Harmer, Rooke & Co.,
   Inc.
3 East 57th St.
New York, NY 10022

Harmers of London
41 New Bond Street
London W1A 4EH
Great Britain

Harmers of New York
6 West 48th St.
New York, NY 10036

Harmers of San Francisco
49 Geary St., Suite 217
San Francisco, CA 94102

Harmers of Sydney
Park House, 9th Floor,
  Suite 3a
187 Macquarie St.
Sydney 2000, Australia

Henrich Stamp Auctions
735 S. W. St. Clair
Portland, OR 97205

Huntington Stamp &
  Coin, Inc.
1060 E. Jericho Turnpike
Huntington, NY 11743

J & M Philatelic Auction
106 W. Broadway St.
Vancouver, BC V5Y 1P3
Canada

John W. Kaufmann
  Auctions
1522 K. St. N. W.
Washington, DC 20005

R. L. Keefe,
302 Lawyers Title
  Building
Tucson, AZ 85701

Daniel F. Kelleher Co.,
  Inc.
10 Post Office Square
Boston, MA 12109

Robert E. Lee, Philatelist
P. O. Box 937
Vernon, BC V1T 6M8
Canada

Robert E. Lippert
  Auctions
23800 Gretaer Mack
St. Clair Shores,
  MI 48080

Greg Manning Auctions,
  Inc.
128 Passaic Ave.
Fairfield, NJ 07006

Metro Stamp Co., Inc.
75-20 Metropolitan Ave.
Middle Village, NY 11379

M. M. Mryczko
14328 Blackman Drive
Rockville, MD 20853

Parcel Poste Company
25 Newtown Rd.
(Route 6)
Danbury, CT 08610

Ram Stamp Company
P. O. Box 3008
Cuyahoga Falls,
  OH 44223

Robbins Auctions, Inc.
147 West 42nd St.
New York, NY 10036

Ed Robertson at Phillips
867 Madison Ave.
New York, NY 10021

Jacques C. Schiff Jr., Inc.
195 Main St.
Ridgefield Park,
  NJ 07660

Simmy's Stamp
  Company, Inc.
148 State St.
Boston, MA 02109

Robert M. Slater, Inc.
14261 E. Fourth Ave.,
  Suite 38
Aurora, CO 80011

Sotheby Parke Bernet
  Stamp Auction Co.,
  Inc.
158 Deer Hill Ave.
Danbury CT 06810

Southeastern Stamp Co.,
  Inc.
1720 Harrison St.
Hollywood, FL 33020

The Stamp Tree, Inc.
701 High St., 216
Auburn, CA 95603

Stampazine
3 East 57th St.
New York, NY 10022

Stereo Stamps
P. O. Box 30035
Chicago, IL 60630

J. & H. Stolow, Inc.
915 Broadway (corner
  21st St.)
New York, NY 10010

Terminal Tower Stamp
  Shop
Main Concourse,
  Terminal Tower
Cleveland, OH 44113

Town & Country Stamps,
  Ltd.
P. O. Box 13542-V
St. Louis, MO 63138

Tropical Stamps, Inc.
P. O. Box 6261
Fort Lauderdale,
  FL 33310

Valley Stamp & Coin
  Center
Valley Mall
Gillette, NJ 07933

Richard Wolffers, Inc.
127 Kearny St.
San Francisco, CA 94108

APPENDIX IX

MAIL-BID SALES

Earl P. L. Apfelbaum,
Inc.
2006 Walnut St.
Philadelphia, PA 19013

Tom Baron
147 West 42nd St.,
Room 617
New York, NY 10036

Buena Park Stamp Co.
P. O. Box 2164
Cypress, CA 90630

Charles Stamp Auctions
Dept. G
P. O. Box 313
Bayside, NY 11361

Chrisco
P. O. Box 452
Miami, FL 33137

Classic Philatelics
P. O. Box 5637
Huntington Beach,
CA 92646

Foster Stamp Sales
1318 Seventh St. N. W.
Albuquerque, NM 87102

Franklin Stamp Co.
2041 M. L. King Ave.,
#400
Washington, DC 20020

Robert Frederic
Collectibles, Inc.
P. O. Box 137
Centereach, Long Island,
NY 11720

Gold Medal Mail Sales
915 Broadway
New York, NY 10010

William J. Hamilton Jr.
P. O. Box 165
Lafayette Hills, PA 19444

Haverlan
P. O. Box 31018
Aurora, CO 80041

Heritage Stamp Gallery
P. O. Box 744 LB
Junction City, KS 66441

Sam Houston Philatelics
14654 Memorial Drive
Houston, TX 77079

ICC
1021 N. La Brea
Los Angeles, CA 90038

JB Enterprises
P. O. Box 529
Cedar Falls, IA 50613

J. L. N. Stamp
P. O. Box 5233
Jersey City, NJ 07305

J. S. Stamps Co.
1318 Custer Ave.
Rockford, IL 61103

J & T Stamps
P. O. Box 182
Poland, NY 13431

Ron Kluger Co.
P. O. Box 22, Gedney
   Station
White Plains, NY 10605

Joseph Lessel Associates
53A Cutter Mill Rd.
Great Neck, NY 11021

Andrew Levitt
P. O. Box 342
Danbury, CT 06810

Linjay Ltd.
P. O. Box 98
Briarcliff Manor,
   NY 10510

Lyn-Co
1615 0 St.
Lincoln, NB 68508

Metro Stamp Co. Inc.
75-20 Metropolitan Ave.
Middle Village, NY 11379

Alan Miller Stamps
1070 East 57th St.
Brooklyn, NY 11234

Minnesota Stamp Co.
P. O. Box 218
Shakopee, MN 55379

Paul Moore Stamps
Route 7
Perryville, MO 63775

PJC Stamps
P. O. Box 272B
Tillsonburg, Ontario
   N4G 4H8 Canada

Norm Postal
P. O. Box 25142
Tamarac, FL 33320

Promenade Stamp Co.
6268 No. Federal
   Highway
Fort Lauderdale,
   FL 33308

Kenneth L. Rice
P. O. Box 6276
W. P. Beach, FL 33405

Oscar V. Rouck
P. O. Box 843
Bemidji, MN 56601

RSA Stamps
P. O. Box 1405
Beverly WV 26253

Charles Russ, Inc.
147 W. 42nd St.
New York, NY 10036

St. George Stamp
   Exchange
P. O. Box 728,
   Downtown Station,
Wichita, KS 67201

Stamps International
P. O. Box 21
Elmhurst, NY 11380

Tippett, Inc.
1469 Main Street
Sarasota, FL 33577

Patrick A. Torchia
2670 North University
   Drive, Suite 202
Sunrise, FL 33322

W. W. Stamp Co.
P. O. Box 587
Columbia, MD 21045

Western Philatelics, Inc.
Del Amo Executive
   Plaza, Suite 107
3868 Carson St.
Torrance, CA 90503

APPENDIX X

ORGANIZATIONS THAT ACCEPT STAMPS AS CHARITABLE DONATIONS

American Philatelic
  Research Library
P. O. Box 338
State College, PA 16801

M. S. Brainard, USVA
Volunteer Service
  (Certified)
Brookings, OR 97415
  (U. S. Navy '08-'21)

Longevity Research
  Foundation
2029 Coolidge St.
Hollywood, FL 33020

Longevity Research
  Foundation
P. O. Box 11135
Chicago, IL 60611

National Philatelic
  Institute
P. O. Box 5942
Chicago, IL 60680

Philatelic Hobbies for the
  Wounded
2122 Wallace Ave.
Bronx, NY 10462

Princeton University
  (College) Library
Lafayette, IN 47907

Stamps for the Wounded
4201 Cathedral Ave.,
  Apt. 815W
Washington, DC 20016